This
BOY

The Early Lives of
John Lennon &
Paul McCartney

This BOY

The Early Lives of
John Lennon &
Paul McCartney

by

Ilene Cooper

VIKING

VIKING

An imprint of Penguin Random House LLC, New York

First published in the United States of America by Viking, an imprint of Penguin Random House LLC, 2023

Visit us online at PenguinRandomHouse.com.

Library of Congress Cataloging-in-Publication Data is available.

ISBN 9780451475855

1st Printing

Printed in the United States of America

LSCH

Book design by Jim Hoover
Text set in Charter Roman, Recoleta Alt Black, and Magazine Grotesque

This is a work of nonfiction. Some names and identifying details have been changed.

For Bill

All You Need Is Love

★ CONTENTS ★

PROLOGUE

July 6, 1957

IT WAS A fine day for a garden party. St. Peter's Church, located in a suburb of Liverpool, England, opened its grounds each year for the fun-filled affair. John Lennon, sixteen years old, was there. He didn't know it, but he had a decision to make that day. He could never have guessed how it would change his life—and the world of music.

John, intense and clever, had formed a skiffle band with some friends. It was called the Quarry Men, after John's school, Quarry Bank. Skiffle was a homegrown folk music, played with an assortment of instruments that could range from a guitar to a bucket with strings attached to a stick that made a thumping bass sound. John liked skiffle, but what he really wanted to play was a new kind of music that was sweeping the United States and making its way across the ocean to England. It was called rock and roll.

What the Quarry Men lacked in real talent they made up for in enthusiasm. Their one standout member was John. He played the guitar with more flair than skill, but he had something just as important as musical ability—star power. John knew how to joke with an audience, grab their attention, and show them a good time. Everyone in the band looked to him as their leader. John would never have settled for anything less.

The garden party, or fête, as the British called it, wasn't fancy, but it delighted guests with floats, game booths, even the crowning of a Rose Queen. And, of course, there was music. Surrounding the stage were folks of all ages, tots to grandparents, clapping and singing along as the Quarry Men played. Also in the audience was a fifteen-year-old boy decked out in a light-colored jacket streaked with silvery strands and skinny black pants. His name was Paul McCartney.

Paul was there with a school friend, Ivan Vaughn; Ivan was also a pal of John's, and he wanted the boys to meet. He knew they both loved rock and they both played the guitar, and Ivan thought Paul might make a good addition to the Quarry Men. Paul was a little nervous about meeting the bandmates, all of whom were older than him. But as he watched them play, Paul noticed something that calmed him down. He was a better musician than any of them.

Paul met the Quarry Men during a break, grabbed a guitar, and started playing. The fresh-faced, dreamy-eyed kid was impressive. He played a song with complicated chord changes called "Twenty Flight Rock" that they never would have attempted.

John looked on and didn't say much, but he was thinking hard. What would letting Paul join the band mean—especially for him? He worried about losing his kingpin status. He pondered what it would take to keep Paul in line. "The decision," he would recall years later, "was whether to keep me strong or make the group stronger. If I take him on, what will happen?"

The aftermath of a German air attack on a Liverpool neighborhood, 1940.

1

Hello, Goodbye

NIGHTTIME IN LIVERPOOL, England, was not just dark; it was a deep, dead black. Outdoor lights were shut off; inside homes and businesses, heavy curtains hid the glow of lamps. When the sky did light up, it was from the bombs Nazi planes were dropping on the city.

England and Germany had been at war since September 1939. For almost a year, there had been little military action. Then, beginning in late August 1940, Germany unleashed a series of powerful air strikes against England, known as the *Blitzkrieg*—the German word for lightning war. Rough-and-tumble Liverpool was one of England's largest seaports, and it was at the bustling docks that food and other supplies arrived from the United States and Canada. Without these necessities, England couldn't hold out against the Nazis. Liverpool was an important city for Germany to break.

The blackout helped hide targets, but Liverpool was being pulverized by the relentless Nazi bombing. Night after night, the sirens would whine, and residents would seek shelter. But even the air-raid shelters weren't safe. One direct hit on a shelter killed 166 people. By the time the air strikes slowed in the spring of 1941, the toll was heavy. Nineteen hundred people died, and many more were injured. Thousands of homes and buildings were destroyed, making life difficult for survivors to carry on, though they did, often with the impudence the city was known for.

In the midst of this chaos, on October 9, 1940, John Lennon was born.

In a burst of patriotism, his mother, Julia, gave him the middle name Winston after England's tireless bulldog of a prime minister, Winston Churchill. When things were looking their darkest for the small island nation, virtually fighting the Nazis alone, it was Churchill's inspiring words that gave England the heart to continue.

Julia's eldest sister, Mary, known by everyone as Mimi, had been waiting for news of the baby's birth. As soon as she heard from the Liverpool Maternity Hospital, she ran through the rubble-strewn streets to be at Julia's side and meet the seven-pound, seven-ounce boy, whom she pronounced "such a beautiful baby." Coming from a family of five sisters, Mimi was delighted that Julia's baby was a boy.

John's father, Alfred Lennon, was not there. A ship's steward in the merchant marines, he was far away at sea. From the first, John had two mothers, really: high-spirited Julia and practical, serious Mimi. But he didn't have a dad. Alf was gone so much, he barely got to see John and Julia.

Julia Stanley and Alf Lennon had met when they were young teenagers in 1928. She was a petite slip of a girl sitting on a Sefton Park bench near a small lake. Alf walked by wearing a round-on-top bowler hat. "You look silly," Alf remembered her saying. He sat down beside her and told her, "You look lovely."

Julia demanded he take his hat off.

Alf promptly tossed it in the water.

That made Julia laugh. Likable Alf was hard to resist.

They started dating, but Alf decided his future would be—as it always had been for so many Liverpool men—sailing the world. Maybe it was because he was a restless dreamer, maybe it was because he was put in an orphanage at age seven after his father's death, but Alf didn't like staying in one place. He wanted to be on the stage, as his father had once been, but despite his good looks and some talent, the more practical plan was to become a seaman. Ocean liners regularly left the Liverpool port before the war, and in 1930, Alf got a job as waiter aboard one of the luxury cruisers.

For most young couples, all the time away and the distance between them would have meant the end of their relationship, but Julia and Alf plodded along. When Alf did return to Liverpool, though, they had good times. The young couple had a lot in common, including a wicked sense of humor, a preference for doing things their own way, and a sharp disdain for authority.

Another thing they shared was a love of music.

Both of them had good singing voices. Julia's was sweet and low. Alf liked to ham it up when he sang, doing imitations of popular singers. Dancing was fun, and they were good at it, even though Alf had worn braces as a kid to straighten his legs. Born into a poor family, he'd contracted rickets, a disease that twisted bones, from not getting the proper nutrients. When Alf was home on shore leave, he and Julia often went to the local clubs to do the dances of the day, like the Savoy Swing and the strutting Lambeth Walk. When it came to instruments, Alf could play the banjo, but Julia could play the banjo, ukulele, accordion, and piano!

You couldn't say that Julia and Alf rushed into marriage. They dated for ten years before they married in December of 1938. He was twenty-six; she was twenty-four. Even then, there might not have been a wedding if Julia's father hadn't been so opposed to the marriage.

Julia's family didn't care for Alf, especially Julia's father, George. In England, where you fit into society was very important, and the Stanleys felt they were a cut above Alfred Lennon, even if it was just a sliver. Alf was a ship's waiter who got jobs on whatever boats happened to be in port, while George, known by everyone as Pop, had been a craftsman, a sailmaker in the days before steam-propelled ships. When his seafaring days were over, he'd settled down with an upright woman, Annie Milward, and worked at a salvage company, lifting sunken ships from the ocean floor. They raised their five girls—Mimi, Elizabeth, Anne, Julia, and Harriet—in the city's rowdy dock area until they were able to move to a small row house on Newcastle Road in the Wavertree area of Liverpool.

Every time Alf reappeared after a voyage, Pop told Julia to get rid of him, but his orders had the opposite effect on headstrong Julia. After a particularly heated argument with her father, who insisted she cut ties, Julia, instead, dared Alf to marry her, and he agreed.

There were no Stanleys present at the local register's office where the short ceremony took place on December 3, 1938, though Alf's brother Sydney was there as witness. Afterward, the newlyweds had a meal and then went to a movie house for their "honeymoon." That night, Julia returned to Newcastle Road, threw her marriage certificate on the dining room table, and announced, "I've done it."

Almost immediately after the wedding, Alf shipped out again, and Julia continued living at home, working as an usherette at the movie theater where she had spent her wedding evening. Slowly, the family came to accept Alf, even if they still felt Julia could have done much better when it came to choosing a husband. By 1939, wartime rationing was firmly in place, which meant everyday items like gasoline, cloth, and many foods were hard to come by, so Alf's ability to bring—or sometimes steal—items from the ship was welcomed, and how the items were obtained was over-looked.

Once the war started, commercial shipping and ocean travel were se-verely limited. So Alf joined the merchant marines, whose vessels were part of the war effort. Ships like the one Alf sailed on were used to deliver goods in and out of England. These ships were important targets for Ger-man U-boats, which tried to sink them or capture their cargo. So even though Alf was just a steward—a step up from waiter—he was often in danger. Still, the money was decent, and after John was born, Alf sent most of it home to cover his family expenses.

Baby John was brought from the hospital to his grandparents' house on 9 Newcastle Road. Even as the Blitz began to slow down, the war raged on, military casualties continued to rise, and the deprivation continued. People in Liverpool tried to find whatever gaiety they could to make their lives more bearable. The United States entered the war in December 1941. Soon the city was filled with lonely American soldiers and sailors, many of whom were looking for a good time to block out the horrors they had been through—or were about to face. Julia, who had taken a job as a barmaid, enjoyed going out in the evening to have a drink or a laugh with service-men, American and British. Alf had told her she should have a good time while he was gone. So she did.

Men liked Julia Lennon, and she liked men. Pretty, with brown eyes and wavy, auburn hair, Julia was also fun to be around. She was cheeky— she could joke and tease—and her high spirits were infectious, making her a bright spot in a very gray world. A relative once said Julia could walk out of a burning house with a smile on her face. Did she enjoy being a mother? Perhaps, but apparently not as much as she enjoyed being out and about, having fun. That left John's care, a good deal of the time, to family. His grandmother Annie died in 1941, but Julia's sisters, occasionally Alf's brother Sydney and his wife, and especially Mimi took up the slack. John did have one clear, sweet memory of that time: Julia singing him the song "I'm Wishing" from the Disney film *Snow White and the Seven Dwarfs* as they cuddled.

Then, in 1943, with the war still raging, Alf deserted the merchant marines. Some say he just was tired of serving. He claimed it was all a mix-up and he had had trouble making it back to his ship. At one point, in the eighteen months he was away, Alf spent time in a naval jail in Algeria for stealing cargo.

The first Julia knew about any of Alf's troubles was when the checks stopped coming. She and toddler John still had a roof over their heads, thanks to Pop, but things were getting very uncomfortable for Julia, whose family was angry with the carefree way she was living her life. This anger boiled over in 1944, when Julia became pregnant by one of her soldier friends, Taffy Williams.

When Alf finally arrived home on one of his rare leaves, he was shocked to learn his wife was going to have a baby by another man. Still, he loved Julia enough to say he would raise the child as his own. Julia, fully aware that her marriage had long been over, said no. Finally, it was Pop Stanley who put his foot down. He was horrified by the situation. Julia being pregnant by one man while married to another was a stain on the family name. He insisted she put the baby up for adoption, and she agreed. The little girl Julia named Victoria, for the coming successful

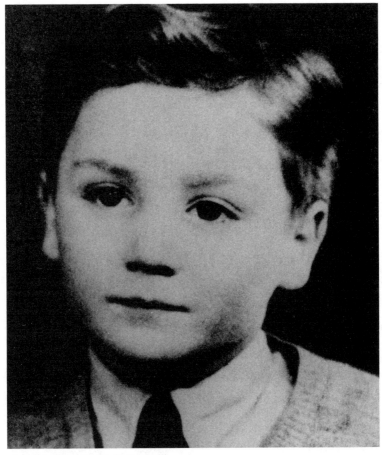

John Lennon, around six years old.

end to the war, was born in 1945 and raised by a Norwegian couple, who changed her name to Ingrid Marie.

By this time, John was almost five. His young life hadn't been easy. Smart and curious, John probably understood that a baby was on the way, in part because there were family fights about the pregnancy. It must have been confusing when Victoria, who was with Julia for several weeks before her adoption, suddenly disappeared. It was only when John was in his twenties that his aunt Harriet resurrected the long-buried memory of his half sister. They never met.

When it was time for John to go kindergarten, he was enrolled in the Mosspits Lane Infant School. By April of the next year, 1946, the five-year-old had been expelled. How naughty do you have to be to be expelled from kindergarten? John, the teachers said, had behavior problems. He liked to frighten the other children, popping out of bushes and yelling at them. He pushed kids around, and their parents complained. The school simply couldn't control him.

But a much more traumatic experience than being dismissed from school awaited John. During the summer of 1946, Alf came back to England for good. The war was over now, and he could make plans for his life. Despite all evidence to the contrary, Alf still had dreams of patching things up with Julia, and he hoped they and John could live together like a proper family.

Julia, however, had moved on. She hadn't bothered to get a divorce but was now living with a man named Bobby Dykins, a waiter at the fanciest hotel in Liverpool. She had no desire to get back together with Alf, who must have seemed like more of a memory than a husband by this time. Then Alf learned that John did not like his "new daddy." The boy had even run away to Mimi's house to get away from Bobby.

So Alf devised a plan. Step one was to take John on a trip to the seaside resort town of Blackpool. Mimi didn't want to let him go, but Julia was out of town, and she didn't feel she had the right to say no to the boy's father.

To five-year-old John, Blackpool must have seemed like heaven, especially after dreary Liverpool, still trying to rebuild after the war. Besides the pure pleasure of running through the waves and playing in the sand, there was a roller coaster, a Ferris wheel, and a boardwalk where you could buy candy and ice cream cones. There were donkey rides! And for the first time, he was really getting to know his father, who was happy to indulge John in every way.

What no one knew was that there was a second step to Alf's plan. The way he figured it, Julia wasn't a great mother, his son didn't like her new boyfriend, and there wasn't much to lure Alf back to Liverpool. He had a pal who was moving to New Zealand. Why shouldn't he and John go with Alf's friend and start a new life, far away, where they could be happy together?

The key element of his scheme was not to tell Julia about any of it.

It was Mimi who first caught on to something being amiss. She nosed around, perhaps talked to Alf's brother, and learned that father and son might not be coming back. She had no right to stop them, but Julia did. Upon her sister's return, Mimi insisted she go to Blackpool get John back. When Julia arrived at the house where Alf and John were staying, she left her boyfriend, Bobby, at the gate, while she went in to talk to Alf. There are several accounts of what took place next, but according to Alf, the conversation soon became heated, and John was sent to the kitchen until things were sorted out.

But Julia and Alf couldn't sort them out. They each had their own idea of where John should end up, and there was no room for compromise between New Zealand and Liverpool. Finally, they came up with the worst idea imaginable, although neither of them seemed to realize it.

They would let five-year-old John make the decision about his future.

John was called in from the kitchen and ran to sit on his father's lap. Alf explained to John that he had to choose. He could sail off to New Zealand with him or return to Liverpool with his mother.

John's mind must have been racing. He loved his mother. She was kind and lively. But she always seemed to be handing him off to someone else. He wasn't fond of Bobby, who was standing outside the door.

John didn't know his father very well, but they had had lots of fun together at the seaside. And John had always wanted to sail on a ship

Blackpool, a seaside resort on the western shore of England, has delighted visitors since the late 1800s.

like those he had seen gliding in and out of Liverpool harbor.

"You!" he said, turning on Alf's lap and pointing to his father. "I want to stay with you."

"Are you sure, John?" Julia asked.

"Leave him be, Julia," Alf demanded. "He wants to stay with me."

Julia didn't argue. She said goodbye and sadly walked out the door.

Within seconds, John realized what he had done. He jumped from Alf's lap and raced out the door to catch Julia. She was his mother. He couldn't bear to let her leave.

Now it was Alf's turn to simply let the boy go. He had offered John a chance to come with him to a place where they could really be father and son. John wanted to stay in England? So be it. Alf watched as his son walked away.

It would be more than fifteen years before they would set eyes on each other again.

Strawberry Fields Forever

JOHN RETURNED WITH Julia and Bobby to the small apartment they shared in Gateacre Village, but he didn't stay there for long.

By September 1946, John was enrolled in Dovedale elementary school near his aunt Mimi's house in the tree-lined suburb (or village, as it was known) of Woolton, where he now lived with Mimi and her husband, George Smith.

What had happened? After dramatically taking John home from Blackpool, why did Julia so quickly give up her son? There are no certain answers, but several possibilities. By August, Julia was pregnant again. Julia Dykins, John's half sister, would be born in March 1947. With a child of his own on the way, Bobby may not have wanted to stretch his resources, financial and emotional, caring for John.

Family pressure was an issue, too. Pop Stanley was once again disapproving of his daughter's choices, and Mimi was already on record as thinking that Julia and Bobby's lifestyle was bordering on scandalous. Since Julia had not divorced Alf, she and Bobby were not only living "in sin," as Mimi thought of it; they were also having a child out of wedlock.

And then there was the matter of John's living conditions. The boy didn't even have his own bed at the Dykins apartment, and Mimi had already reported this fact to the local social services agency. Social workers investigated and strongly suggested that Julia make other arrangements for John. Now, with a baby on the way, Mimi was ready to press the issue again, and Julia might have decided that fighting family and the authorities was just too much to handle.

John's cousin and childhood playmate Leila was a witness to perhaps the final sharp argument between her aunts Julia and Mimi, ending with a declaration. "I remember Mimi standing in front of John and telling Julia, 'You're not having him!'" Distressingly, for the second time in John's young life, he was present for a tug-of-war over his future.

Whatever the reasons, or combinations of them, it was decided once and for all that John would be better off living with Aunt Mimi and her husband, George.

So the confusion over John's upbringing was finally settled. But the stability that came with his small upstairs room at the front of the house and the smell of fresh-baked apple tarts that wafted up from Mimi's kitchen had a price. Mimi was determined to turn John into the well-mannered, high-achieving boy that she wanted him to be.

Mary Stanley Smith, known to everyone as Mimi, was not the sort of person you said no to. The words used to describe her by family and friends included *sharp, no-nonsense,* and *firm.* That didn't mean she didn't have a sense of humor, however. All five of the Stanley sisters knew how to have a laugh. Sometimes, a friend later remembered, John and his aunt would be squabbling, and "the next moment you'd find them rolling around, laughing together." But, for Mimi, laughs came after responsibilities.

As the eldest Stanley sister, Mimi had helped take care of her four younger sisters when they were growing up, which was enough mothering for her. She didn't even want to get married, an unusual decision for women in those days, choosing instead to become a nurse, then working her way up to manage a hospital ward. When she grew tired of that, she became personal secretary to a wealthy businessman.

Mimi's husband, George, had owned a dairy farm with his brothers and delivered the milk to the hospital where Mimi worked during her nursing days. She caught his eye, and they started dating. Mimi was content to let the courtship go on indefinitely. Like Julia and Alf's, Mimi and George's relationship continued for years, and it was only when George put his foot down and told Mimi it was either marriage or nothing that she agreed to marry him, before the outbreak of the war in 1939.

Children didn't seem to be in their future. There was an exception, though. Mimi's niece Leila said later that Mimi had never wanted children, "but she wanted John." From her first look at baby John the day he was born, Mimi had felt an attachment to the little boy. After watching for years with dismay—and sometimes horror—at the way Julia was caring for her son, Mimi was more than happy to finally take over the job permanently.

Mimi and George were determined to give John stability in the very nice home George had inherited. It was called Mendips, after the rolling Mendips Hills in the Somerset area of England. Much of Liverpool, especially the city center, had been bombed out during the war, but the suburban Woolton area was relatively untouched. With housing at a great premium in postwar Liverpool, Mendips, a semidetached three-bedroom

Mendips, built in 1933, was home to John from ages five through his early twenties, though in later years he was often traveling or staying with friends.

house located at 251 Menlove Avenue, was considered a real prize.

Though it faced a busy street, the stucco house, built in 1933, was quite charming, with decorative leaded-glass windows and a good-sized yard where John could play. The front door, with its flower-design stained glass window, was impressive, but most visitors came in through the kitchen because the fastidious Mimi didn't want people tromping through the house. In the cozy morning room, John would have his meals, including his favorite: eggs and chips—what the British call french fries. The first floor also featured a dining room and living room, also known as the lounge. Both looked out on Mimi's side garden, where she and George enjoyed growing flowers, gooseberries, blackberries, and red currants. When he got older, John got five shillings a week to mow the grass around the garden, which, by all reports, he did quickly and poorly.

Inside the house, there were other appealing features: an art deco–style fireplace and built-in bookshelves. Attached to a wall was a bell board that allowed the residents to ring for the maid that the house builder expected the occupants would employ. Mimi and George never had servants, but it was a fancy touch. Appearances were important to Mimi, and living in the pretty village of Woolton in a comfortable home made her feel that she was now very firmly in the middle class.

John, who went from having no bed with the Dykinses to his own bedroom, must have enjoyed having a space of his own, even though it was small. There was just enough room for a narrow bed, a dresser, and a desk, but the bay window over the desk looked past Menlove Avenue to the expansive green of a golf course.

As a small boy, John would head off to bed with his stuffed animals, a panda and a teddy bear, tucked under his arms. When he got a little older, he would sit at his desk, sometimes writing, sometimes drawing. A speaker hooked up to the radio downstairs played the pleasant popular music Mimi and George liked in the background.

Having stayed many times with his aunt and uncle, little John settled in easily, at least physically, but he still had to deal with the abrupt parting from his parents. As an adult he remembered, "I soon forgot my father. It was like he was dead. But I did see my mother now and again, and my feeling never died off for her."

Although Mimi allowed Julia to stop by once in a while or visit with John at family gatherings, she didn't want his mother to play any real role in his life. She told the young boy that Julia lived far away, and that's why he couldn't see her very often. The truth was, the house where she lived with Bobby, little Julia, and, later, another daughter, Jackie, who was born in 1949, was only a couple of miles from Mendips, on the other side of the golf course.

John with his mother, Julia, at a family gathering in 1949. She is pregnant with his half sister Jackie.

Mimi claimed, after John had become famous, that the boy was "as happy as the day was long." That may have been true in some respects, but inwardly, he struggled tremendously with the fact that he wasn't living with his mother while his sisters were. He once asked Mimi why he still called Julia "Mummy" and called her Mimi. "Well, you couldn't have two mummies, could you?" Mimi replied, without really answering the underlying question of why he, unlike anyone else he knew, had two mother figures.

Even as an adult, his childhood haunted him. He was almost thirty when he wrote the song "Mother," which he sang with deep, almost savage emotion. "You had me / But I never had you . . . Father . . . I needed you / you didn't need me."

Eight-year-old John (far right) with his cousins David, Leila, and Michael and his half sister Julia Dykins.

Life with Mimi and George couldn't have been more different for John than the one he had known. Now he had two people in the role of parents willing to revolve their lives around him. Mimi was proud that she—unlike Julia, who was often out in the evening—rarely left home at night. Silver-haired George, who might have been expected to balk at the responsibility of a little boy, seemed to take to instant fatherhood with enthusiasm. After Pop Stanley died when John was eight, George was the only male father figure in his life, and by every report, he was a sweet, kind man devoted to John. There was no question that George was far more easygoing with the boy than Mimi was.

Mimi insisted that John only go to the movies once in the summer to see the latest Disney film like *Cinderella*. At Christmastime, the family went to one of Liverpool's theaters to see the annual Christmas pantomime, a live show with singing, dancing, and lots of jokes. But George thought two outings a year wasn't enough, and he would sneak John into movies, with Mimi none the wiser. He supplemented the single piece of hard candy Mimi allowed with smuggled bars of chocolate, and even though Mimi refused to go out at night, it was George who tucked John in. When it came to affection, George was the adult with whom young John would exchange *squeakers*—their word for kisses.

If Mimi wanted to provide stability, she succeeded, and John knew she loved him, even if she wasn't the hugging type. But sometimes her high standards seemed like a noose around John's neck. He was expected to toe the line, and though she spanked only as a last resort when he was bad, she often gave him the cold shoulder, which he hated. "Don't 'nore me, Mimi," the little boy would plead when she was displeased with his actions.

Even as life grew into a pleasant routine, John was still dealing with his anger and insecurities, which Mimi didn't seem to want to acknowledge. That led the boy to only mostly behave when he was under her watchful eye. However, when he was in school or out playing with friends, especially as he got older, a quite different and very difficult John emerged.

Inside the house, John was a bright, curious boy who spent his time reading, writing, and drawing. Mimi was a great reader, and the house was filled with books. If she had extra money, she spent it at the bookstore. John learned to read early on by sitting on George's lap, picking out words from the local newspaper, the *Liverpool Echo*. Soon he began to devour books.

He delighted in everything from *The Wind in the Willows*, which featured Mole, Ratty, and Mr. Toad and their adventures in the English countryside, to the Just William stories about a rambunctious boy, the leader of a gang of friends who named themselves the Outlaws. John saw a lot of himself in William.

His favorite book, though, was Lewis Carroll's *Alice in Wonderland*, which he read and reread. As an adult, he remembered, "I was passionate about *Alice in Wonderland* and drew all the characters." He was particularly fascinated by the wordplay in the Alice books, especially in the poems "The Walrus and the Carpenter" and "Jabberwocky," from the Alice sequel, *Through the Looking-Glass*. "Jabberwocky" begins, "'Twas brillig, and the slithy toves / did gyre and gimble in the wabe . . ."

Captivated by both words and images in the poetry, John tried his hand at each.

The long-running Just William series featuring a swaggering eleven-year-old was a favorite of British schoolchildren.

John was still in primary school when he began to write his own small books. He had one series called Sport, Speed and Illustrated, edited and illustrated by J. W. Lennon. With self-assurance, he ended each one by noting, "If you liked this one, come again next week and it will be even better." Mimi remembered, "He never had a pencil out of his hand. He'd write something down, then screw up the bit of paper and throw it away and start again. And then he'd say, 'You ought to pick these up, Mimi, because I'm going to be famous one day, and they'll be worth something.'"

Mimi also looked out for John's spiritual life. She enrolled him in the Sunday school at St. Peter's, a nearby Anglican church, an impressive building built from locally quarried sandstone. When he grew older, John would sing in the church choir. But he broke at least one of the Ten Commandments there, because it was also the place where John taught his pals how to steal money out of the collection plate for bubble gum.

It was just this kind of behavior that made John unpopular with his friends' parents. "Keep away from him," John said much later, repeating what he knew was a common opinion. "The parents instinctively recognized what I was, which was a troublemaker."

Though Mimi kept a strict eye on John while he was around the house, she couldn't follow him to school. She did try in the beginning. She'd trail him to make sure he made it safely until an embarrassed John put up a fuss. John soon made it his mission to flee Mimi's prying eyes whenever he could.

There was one place of escape that sparked John's young imagination and left a deep impression on him. It was called Strawberry Field, although the neighbors commonly added an *s*, making it Strawberry Fields.

The original Strawberry Field and the Victorian house that dominated the grounds were gifted to the Salvation Army in the mid-1930s. It functioned as a children's home for seventy years.

A short walk from Mendips, Strawberry Fields was the picturesque name for a Salvation Army orphanage. The Gothic-style mansion that housed the fifty or so children who lived there sat in the middle of a park-like setting. In the summer, Strawberry Fields would open its strawberry-red gates and host garden parties with homemade treats, game stalls, and lemonade stands. Mimi remembered years later that when a young John heard the Salvation Army band start playing, "he'd pull me along saying, 'Hurry up, Mimi! We're going to be late.'"

But the times John relished most at Strawberry Fields came a little later when he was old enough to climb over the orphanage's brick walls and run inside to play with the children. Mimi strongly disapproved, so he had to do it on the sly, but when he would get caught, he would laugh and tell his aunt, "They can't hang you for it." He must have had the sense that though he was surrounded by extended family, like the kids at Strawberry Fields, his life wasn't the norm; he, too, was living without parents.

There were other things that fed into this feeling. Maybe it was his artistic talent, perhaps it was his love affair with books, which took his imagination places that other kids didn't go. Or it could have been that John literally saw things differently because his eyesight was so bad.

John was extremely nearsighted, which means he could see things clearly close up, but farther away, objects and people were blurry, giving him an almost surreal feel to his world. As soon as Mimi realized John was nearsighted, around age seven, she took him to get glasses. The government-issued glasses were plain round ones, with wires for arms that curled uncomfortably around his ears. John hated those glasses. Friends remember him putting on his glasses for the shortest time possible before shoving them in a pocket. Eventually Mimi gave in and bought him a more expensive pair, but even those he would wear only when absolutely necessary.

Without his glasses, John could believe that he lived in a sort of magical world that no one else could see. His awareness that he was different—something special even—became his most important secret.

As an adult, he tied these feelings with his memories of Strawberry Fields. In one line of his song "Strawberry Fields," he wrote, "No one I

Mimi Smith at Mendips in the 1960s.

think is in my tree." John later recalled, "What I was trying to say in that line is nobody seems to be as hip as me. Therefore I must be crazy or a genius . . . It's the same problem that I had when I was five: there is something wrong with me because I seem to see things other people don't see."

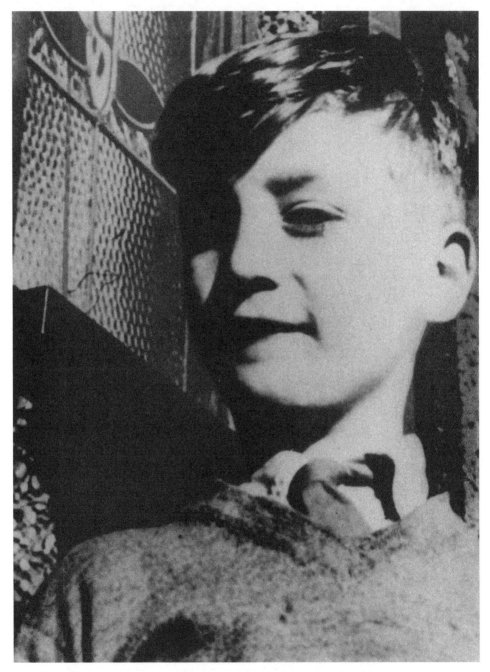

John standing in front of one of Mendips's stained glass windows in 1947.

Bad Boys

JOHN'S FEELINGS ABOUT being special—and his embarrassment about his unusual family life—translated into a specific image. He decided to project a clever, cheeky John Lennon who was daring and above ordinary rules. His self-confidence, along with his wit and generosity, was attractive to other boys, and he soon became the leader of his own gang, just like the Outlaws in the Just William books.

Ivan Vaughn lived behind Mendips on Vale Road. A good student, Ivan was an important part of John's life, as was Nigel Walley, who also lived on Vale Road. Nigel's father was a policeman, so the boys had to keep a lot of their mischief hidden from him. John's best friend, though, was another neighborhood boy, slightly younger, with curly, white-blond hair—Pete Shotton.

Their relationship did not get off to a good start. Six-year-old Pete found that he could drive John wild by making fun of his middle name, not just calling him Winston, but Winnie, like Winnie-the-Pooh. Finally, John told Pete he'd better stop—or else. Pete chose "or else." He lunged at John, and a fight began. John, seven, was bigger and stronger. Once John had Pete pinned down, he made him promise no more Winnie.

Pete agreed, got up, danced away, and promptly yelled, "Winnie, Winnie, Winnie!"

John was furious—but suddenly he started laughing. He had to admire someone who stood up to him, especially after a fistfight. After that, John and Pete became inseparable friends, so much so that they were known around Woolton as Lotton or Shennon, nicknames coined by John himself, another example of the way he had fun with words.

Although Liverpool proper was still gritty—the local paper used words like *slovenly, filthy,* and *dilapidated* to describe it—out in pleasant Woolton, John was living in a boy's paradise. He and his pals had plenty of open space to play and hang out.

A favorite spot was Foster's Field, a deserted property surrounded by walls of local sandstone. Once the high walls were climbed, the boys had the place all to themselves. The chief attraction was a murky pond that was home to weeds, insects, and frogs, which the boys would try to catch. John and Pete had been warned by Mimi and Pete's mother to stay away from the potentially dangerous pond. Instead, they put together a small raft, which they used to paddle through the water. "The construction," Pete recalled later, "was somewhat flawed—perhaps because we built it ourselves—so we often ended up wringing wet." When that happened, the boys had to build a fire to dry their clothes—and themselves—so they could return home without their families knowing what they'd been up to.

John and his gang of Outlaws, now nine and ten years old, had plenty of other ideas that caused their parents no end of grief. The boys would throw chunks of dirt down on people from a bridge, shoplift when they could, and sneak into the golf course John could see from his bedroom window to annoy the golfers. Some of the boys' activities were dangerous, like jumping onto the bumpers of the trams that chugged up and down Menlove Avenue, hanging on for dear life.

As they had when he was younger, parents told their children to stay away from John Lennon. An unrepentant adult John understood why. "I did not conform and [they thought] I would influence their kids, which I did. I did my best to disrupt every friend's home I had. Partly, maybe, it was out of envy that I didn't have this so-called home. But I really did. I had an auntie and uncle and a nice suburban home."

Not being raised in a conventional home environment may have bothered John, but it also freed him. "Anyway," he continued, "the fact that I wasn't with my parents made me see that parents aren't gods . . . That was the gift of not having parents. I cried a lot about not having them, and it was torture, but it gave me awareness, early."

This mix of pride and shame continued to entangle itself with John's ongoing perception that he was special. "I was always so psychic or intuitive or poetic or whatever you want to call it, that I was always seeing things in a hallucinatory way. It was scary as a child because there was nobody to relate to. Neither my auntie nor my friends, nor anybody, could ever see what I did . . . I saw loneliness."

John's complex way of seeing the world translated into his everyday life, sometimes in unfortunate ways. There was a cruel streak to John that grew more pronounced as he got older. He had a fascination with physical abnormalities and was always using his considerable artistic skills to draw people and animals with no limbs, too many limbs, covered with warts. He would break up his friends by doing imitations of physical deformities or pretending he had claws instead of hands. John could also be a bully and cruel to other kids. Even John's friends weren't immune from his need to impose his will on people. Pete tells the story of the time John kept tapping him on the head with a bicycle pump just to anger him. "Getting the egg, are you? Getting the egg, then, Shotton?" John said, repeating over and over the Liverpool slang for getting mad.

Mimi must have known about this "outside" John, but she tried to convince herself that the boy who read and discussed books with her in the morning room wasn't also the neighborhood bad boy. Once, though, she did come face-to-face with her nephew's wilder side.

"I was coming down Penny Lane one day and I saw this crowd of boys in a ring, watching two boys fighting." She thought to herself, *Just like those common Rose Lane scruffs*. But when the fight ended, "out came this awful boy with his coat hanging off. To my horror, it was Lennon."

John didn't mind at all when Mimi told that story, saying, "Just like you, Mimi. Everybody else is always common." He was pleased to show her that he wasn't the perfect gentlemen she was trying so hard to raise.

John's tempestuous personality and the unsettled feelings he had about himself were soothed by a couple things that seemed to make him completely happy: his musical ability and his summer trips with his cousins to Scotland.

After the war ended in 1945, the Smith family dairy business was sold. That left George to scramble for work, eventually winding up with a series of low-paying jobs and a side business as a bookie, taking bets on horses. Technically, that kind of off-track betting was illegal, though the police usually ignored it. Mimi hated George's involvement with gambling, which she thought was an embarrassment. To stretch the family budget, Mimi decided they should rent out Mendips's third bedroom to college students.

She preferred renting to veterinary students because they could keep tabs on the family dog, Sally, and beloved pet cats Tich, Tim, and Sam, a Persian that John had found wandering outside.

One of those students, Harold Phillips, played the harmonica. John, about eleven at the time, was fascinated by the instrument, and Harold, impressed by the boy's persistent questions, told him if he could play a song by the next day, he would give him the harmonica. As unlikely as that seemed, the following afternoon, a confident John played not one but two songs. Aunt Mimi insisted the harmonica be given as a Christmas gift, but the anticipation only heightened John's excitement. "I felt the stocking and there was a mouth organ in it. A harmonica. That was one of the great moments of life, when I got my first harmonica."

With all the trouble Mimi had taming John, she was probably as pleased as he was when it came time for his Scottish summer vacations. Mimi and Julia's sister Elizabeth, a widow with a son named Stanley, married a dentist, Bertie Sutherland, who opened a dental practice in Edinburgh. Starting when John was about eight, John's cousin Stanley, seven years older, would fetch him and bring him to Scotland. Stanley remembered, "He'd stay there for a week or so and then off we'd go up to the Sutherland family croft [a small, rustic farm] up in Durness at Cape Wrath, which is the most fartherly northwest tip of Scotland."

John was entranced with the dramatic Scottish scenery, a far cry from both the grittier parts of Liverpool and its sedate suburb, Woolton. The air was crisp and clean, the foliage grew rough and wild, and a sandy beach hugged a scenic bay. Best of all, there was no Mimi breathing down his neck. "John just loved the wildness and the openness of the place," Stanley remembered. "We went fishing and hunting, and John loved going up into the hills to draw or write poetry."

John with his cousins Stanley and Leila.

A few years later, John was allowed to start taking the bus to Scotland alone. It was on one of these journeys that the bus driver heard John playing his harmonica. He told John that someone had left a harmonica on the bus, which he'd turned in to the lost and found. If it was still there, the bus driver told John, he could have it. It was there, and now a thrilled John owned an even better harmonica than the one he'd been gifted by Harold. John's musical talents also got a boost when Stanley taught him to play the accordion, which John picked up as easily as he did the harmonica. The folk song "Greensleeves" was his signature tune.

Even though John seemed calmer and more relaxed in Scotland, he could be a trickster. One local girl whose family owned the village shop remembered how John enjoyed practical jokes. "He loved picking up seaweed from the sea and tying it to the doors outside the store so we couldn't get out."

Regular vacations with his relatives ended when John was in his teens, but he would still go up north for the occasional visit. For the rest of his life, John had a great affection for Scotland and the freedom it had offered him as a boy.

There was one activity in Woolton that gave John a similar feeling of being on his own and in charge of his own doings, and that was riding his bicycle, either alone or with friends. For young people in 1950s England, the key to independence was a bicycle. Even as grown-up, John remembered the excitement of his first bike, a sturdy Raleigh Lenton. "As a kid I had a dream—I wanted my own bicycle. When I got the bike I must have been the happiest kid in Liverpool, maybe the world. I lived for that bike."

John could often be seen riding around Woolton, past the church, through the hilly parks, over to the shopping area called Penny Lane. Unfortunately, between his refusal to wear his glasses and his propensity for daydreaming, biking could be dangerous. To Pete's horror, he once watched as John rode right into the back of a parked car. "John was catapulted off his bike and over the car's roof. In a virtuoso display of his catlike resilience, however, John managed to land in the middle of the road, squarely on his feet." The beloved bike was in worse shape than John, who had a few scrapes; the bicycle had a dented rim. Happily, they were able to drag it home, fix up John's bruises, and hammer out the dents.

By 1950, John's days at Dovedale Primary School were counting down. The British government had mandated difficult tests, called the eleven-plus exams, for all children of that age to take. How you did on the tests would decide whether you continued your education at vocational school for learning a trade, a secondary school for average academic students, or a grammar school for the brightest. Where a child went to school almost always determined where they would wind up in

England's rigid class system. It wasn't easy to move ahead, but having a good education helped, especially for those whose families were trying to become solidly middle class.

John passed his eleven-plus examination with flying colors, even though he didn't study for it. His love of reading—his favorite authors were now Edgar Allan Poe; the humorist James Thurber; and Robert Louis Stevenson, who wrote *Treasure Island*—gave him an edge when it came to test taking. There were several fine grammar schools in Liverpool, the best being the Liverpool Institute. But Mimi chose nearby Quarry Bank for John, in part because it had a reputation for being strong on discipline, something that even she realized John needed at this point.

In September 1951, John, along with Pete, entered Quarry Bank High School for Boys. Pete described the six-year school as "an ivy-covered brick fortress." Their uniforms were similar to those worn at Dovedale: blazer, white shirt, tie, and short pants. (Older boys got to wear trousers.) The blazers sported an emblem with a red-and-gold stag's head, the school symbol.

The teachers, called masters, wore long Hogwarts-style gowns and took their job seriously—to mold their students into upstanding young men. John Lennon came to Quarry Bank with a different agenda. He was going to take nothing seriously and intended to have as much fun as possible. As he had at Dovedale, John became a leader of the boys in his grade, and with Pete at his side, he was soon in no end of trouble. Infractions of the rules earned students black marks, and "Lotton" were soon piling them up, leading to suspensions and the occasional serious paddling by the headmaster. Decades later, someone at the school came across the Lennon infraction book, full of black marks, and sold it at auction for lots of money when John became famous!

John and Pete put time and effort into their disruptions. Their pranks included hiding alarm clocks to go off during class and rigging blackboards to fall down. Once, standing behind an elderly master named Mr. Galloway after class, John boldly tickled the few white hairs on the master's nearly bald head while Pete looked on. When Galloway, thinking it was a fly, would try to swat it away, John hid his hand, only to start the game all over after the teacher turned his attention back to his papers. The boys were doubled up with suppressed laughter, but something had to give. John found the whole thing so funny, he peed his pants. Hearing a *drip, drip, drip* and noticing a puddle on the floor, Mr. Galloway looked around and asked, "What the devil is that?" Without missing a beat, John replied, "I think the roof is leaking, sir." By their second year at Quarry Bank, John and Pete had slipped from the A stream, classes for the best students, to B. The year after that, it was down to C.

There's no doubt that John drove the masters crazy. In the teachers' lounge, among themselves, a few did acknowledge his charisma, intelligence, and artistic talent—which they also noted were being put to very bad use. They were especially impressed—once it had been confiscated—by a book John created called *The Daily Howl*. Each new installment consisted of art, verse, or both and was eagerly passed around among the students. Playing on the popularity of American frontiersman Davy Crockett, John wrote "The Story of Davy Crutch-Head." It had weather reports: "Tomorrow will be Muggy. Followed by Tuggy, Wuggy, and Thuggy." One of his drawings featured a blind man in dark glasses being led by a blind dog, also wearing dark glasses. John's fascination with depicting physical differences would continue well into adulthood. *The Daily Howl* was a visible example of so many of his traits: wit, creativity, and confidence, with a streak of cruelty.

Perhaps John and Pete's most ambitious prank involved the British holiday Guy Fawkes Day, which commemorates a failed plot to blow up the Houses of Parliament. The November 5 holiday is celebrated with bonfires burning all over England. In Woolton, as in previous years, a huge bonfire was planned. The young people of Woolton had spent several weeks collecting great amounts of wood, old furniture, and newspapers and bringing them to an area known as the Tip, near John's house.

The huge pile of stacked wood was ready the day before the holiday. John got the bright idea to light it as a joke. Pete ran home to get matches, and the boys, along with a few friends, set it ablaze. Not really thinking ahead, they hadn't considered that the residents of Woolton, who had been looking forward to the Guy Fawkes Day celebration, would be furious that someone (or someones) had ruined all the fun.

Sure enough, as the bonfire began raging, angry people poured out of their homes. The kids who'd collected all that wood were especially mad that their hard work was literally turning to ashes. As Pete recalled, "Our sense of triumph soon gave way to one of stark trepidation; were we to be caught out this time, our standing in the community would have made Jack the Ripper seem enviable by comparisons." One local tough told Pete if he ever found who did it, he would kill him. Luckily, he never learned the truth.

When John was about fourteen, his complicated family life was twisted once more. John was still under the impression that Julia lived some distance away, with Bobby Dykins and their two daughters. His cousin Stanley, now a young man, was tired of the deception and decided the time had come for John to know the truth. One day, without telling Mimi or the rest of his family, he took John to Julia's house at 1 Bloom-field Road in the suburb of Allerton, a twenty-minute walk away.

There's no record of how John reacted, either to the revelation or the deception, but as soon as he found out that Julia was so close, he decided that things were going to change. With an exciting sense of new beginnings, he began visiting her regularly, even sleeping over now and then. For her part, Julia was delighted to have John back in her life in a more consistent way. Still full of fun, Julia probably realized she'd never be a mother figure to John— that was Mimi's role. But she could do what Mimi couldn't: indulge him, share his growing interest in music, and support his dreams unconditionally.

As for John, he felt like he'd found a kindred spirit in Julia. When he told her about some of his outrageous behavior, she didn't scold him. She laughed. After all, she was known for her own brand of hijinks, like wearing glasses without lenses while talking to the neighbors and then, deadpan, sticking her finger in the hole to rub her eye. John's skipping school didn't bother her much either. Many a school day, John would wave to Mimi as he was heading to Quarry Bank and then veer off for Julia's house. Sometimes, Pete would join him, and Julia would greet them. "It's lovely to see you. Don't worry about school; don't worry about a thing." John's other friends would come over, too, and they all remember Julia as a one of a kind: pretty, girlish, and unlike any mother they knew.

With more frequent visits, John also got a chance to develop relationships with his two young sisters, Julia and Jacqueline, and Bobby Dykins. By now, most people assumed Julia and Bobby were married, but, in fact, Julia and Alfred had still never divorced. John, in his typical impudent fashion, nicknamed Bobby "Twitchy" because of his sometimes-jerky movements and the way he was always nervously clearing his throat, but John didn't really dislike Bobby. Still a head waiter in one of Liverpool's best hotels, Bobby sometimes let John take a handful of coins from the tip jar he brought home, which John appreciated.

Naturally, Mimi wasn't pleased by this turn of events. It must have been irritating to see Julia getting to enjoy the fun, creative side of John, while

Mimi was dealing with a sullen teenager whose grades were plummeting and whose school reports contained phrases like *wasted intelligence* or *little hope*. Then, in the summer of 1955, something happened that was even worse for Mimi than John's downward slide. Seemingly out of nowhere, George Smith collapsed at Mendips and, though rushed to the hospital, died there of a stomach hemorrhage. John was on his way to Scotland but immediately returned home. "I remember coming home the day Uncle George died . . . Mimi was crying over the carrots . . . I didn't know how to be sad publicly, what you did or said." John hid out in his bedroom. "Then my cousin Leila arrived and she came upstairs as well. We both had hysterics. We just laughed and laughed." Though it's not unusual for young people to react inappropriately and awkwardly when they encounter death for the first time, John always felt guilty about that nervous laughter.

John, however, was not insensitive to Mimi's feelings. While we don't know the backstory, apparently Mimi's sisters, as close as they were, didn't support her in her time of grief the way John felt they should have. So he wrote her a poem, and in it he called her "the best of the five." For all John's infatuation with his new relationship with Julia, he appreciated everything Mimi had done to bring a sense of normalcy to his life. As one biographer of John's put it, "He exasperated her and she infuriated him, but theirs was always an earthy two-way relationship in which both could grow." Until he became famous—and even a bit after—John continued to live at Mendips.

Now that John Lennon was a teenager, his life was more complex than ever. His early life had been confusing, and his future was uncertain. He thought of himself as special but couldn't quite see how his uniqueness would impress the wider world. But the winds of change were blowing hard, and they were clearing a path for rebels like John to make their voices heard.

Mother Nature's Son

"I'LL BUILD A stairway to heaven—with a new step every day!"

Paul McCartney loved that song as a little boy. He loved listening to his father, Jim, sing and tinkle the keys on the family's secondhand piano. The McCartneys moved a lot when Paul was a boy, and while his family may not have always had luxuries (and sometimes practicalities, like an indoor toilet), the houses were always filled with music.

There were four people in the McCartney family: Jim; his wife, Mary; Paul, who was born on June 18, 1942; and Paul's brother, Michael, who arrived two years later. By the time of Paul's birth, the heavy bombing of Liverpool had stopped, but the war was still raging. British soldiers, sailors, and airmen were fighting and dying in great numbers. With America and Russia now in the battle against Nazi Germany, England was a little more hopeful about the war's eventual outcome. But these were still dark days.

Jim, in his late thirties when the war started, was too old to fight, but that didn't mean he hadn't spent the early days of the war in danger. Along with his day job at an aircraft factory, at night he was a fire watcher. Between 1940 and 1941, when the Nazi bombing was at its most brutal, Jim would sit atop Liverpool roofs, protected only by his metal helmet, listening to the bombs make their peculiar tinny whistle as they fell on the city. If one exploded in his neighborhood, it was Jim's job to get in touch with the fire department and then help put out the fires and clear the rubble.

Fire watchers like Jim McCartney clear the rubble after a bombing in Liverpool during the war.

Central Liverpool was a portrait of destruction, a mess of cinders, soot, and crumbling concrete. Residents died when their houses were blown apart or collapsed. Sometimes death or injury came with the impact of flying debris. Being a fire watcher brought Jim face-to-face with the destruction and anguish that his city was enduring.

But once in a while, Jim got a night off. One evening in 1940, Jim was at a party. He had his eye on a friend of one of his sisters, but Jim was worried the party might break up before he had a chance to introduce himself to Mary Mohin.

Parties didn't last too late at night because of the bombings and the blackouts. Even a speck of light could draw the Nazi planes. The festive get-together came to a sudden halt when air-raid sirens went off. The Germans bombers were at it again, and everyone headed to the cellar to wait it out. Being underground provided safety from flying glass or shrapnel, but if there was a direct hit on a building, it could collapse, so being downstairs had its own dangers. This siege was a long one, but something good came of it. Jim and Mary sat on the cellar stairs, talking for hours.

Who knows what they talked about, but Liverpudlians (yes, that's what those who hail from Liverpool are called) were a tight lot, close to their families, so there's a good chance they talked about that.

There had been McCartneys in Liverpool since the 1860s when they'd made their way from Ireland across the Irish Sea, first to Scotland, then to England. Life hadn't been easy for them. Life for immigrants new to a country rarely is.

Paul's great-grandfather had been a plumber. His grandfather Joe spent his days in a factory cutting tobacco leaves, hoping that enough of the excess would fall into his pant cuffs so he could pluck it out and roll his own cigars. He'd sell those to make an extra penny or two, much needed because Joe had a big family to feed. He and his wife, Florrie, had nine children. The seven that lived through childhood grew up in one of the worst parts of Liverpool, a dank and dirty neighborhood, but the family was a loving unit. Joe played the tuba in a military band, and music spilled out of their cramped living quarters. Jim McCartney, born in 1902, was Joe and Florrie's second-oldest child, and the music soaked into his soul.

Jim's first job, at fourteen, was selling programs at a music hall. When people left them after the first show, Jim would scoop them up, run home, and have his sisters iron them so he could sell them again at the next show. A little later, he found work in Liverpool's bustling Cotton Exchange, hauling bales of cotton and samples of cloth around Liverpool to be purchased by textile mills. But if cotton was for the day, the nights were for making music.

As a boy, Jim began playing a banged-up trumpet, and he taught himself to play piano. By eighteen, Jim had started his own band called the Masked Melody Makers—he figured wearing black fabric masks with cut-out eyeholes would get the group some attention. Well, it did when the color from the cheap masks melted in the hot, humid dance halls, dripping down their faces, but other than that, the band didn't go anywhere. Not one to give up, Jim started another band, and this next effort, Jim Mac's Jazz Band, was a popular group around the city in the 1920s and '30s.

But as much as Jim loved music, he saw it as more of a hobby than a career. When his company promoted him from cotton hauler to cotton salesman—an almost unheard-of step up the social ladder for someone from the lower classes—Jim gave up the band. After the war started in 1939, the government took over the cotton industry, and that's when he moved to the aircraft factory.

The dark-haired, soft-eyed Mary Mohin who sat and talked to Jim Mc-

Cartney that night on the cellar steps wasn't a girl. She was thirty-one years old, and in those days, any woman still unmarried by that age was often given the dismissive, mean-spirited nickname *old maid*. It wasn't that Mary had anything against getting married; it was just that she had been busy with something else—her career. Mary was a nurse.

From a young age, Mary knew she might have to take care of herself. Her mother died when she was ten years old. Two years later, her father remarried. The new wife didn't care much for Mary, and Mary didn't like her either, so she moved in with relatives. Some girls would have wilted from these unfortunate circumstances. In Mary, they fired a determination to improve her life. She decided to go to nursing school and started her training at fourteen. When she met Jim, she had already worked for many years as a registered nurse.

When the all-clear signal came after that long chat on the cellar stairs, it was also clear that Jim and Mary wanted to see more of each other. Mary found Jim "charming" and very entertaining. Jim adored Mary and admired her independence. The war made some people jump into marriage. But Jim and Mary were worried that as a nurse, Mary might be asked to work overseas, so they waited almost a year to wed, until her future was more certain. On April 15, 1941, they were married in the chapel at St. Swithin's, a Roman Catholic church. That was Mary's choice; Jim was a Protestant, but he wasn't much interested in religion. Catholics and Protestants marrying could be a divisive issue in Liverpool, where there was sometimes fighting between the two groups. It didn't seem to be a problem for Jim and Mary.

James Paul McCartney—always to be known as Paul—was born the following year on June 18th, and once again the issue of religion was raised. It was Mary's decision again to have him (and later his brother,

Michael, born in 1944) baptized as a Catholic, but it seems she viewed it as more of a formality than a way of raising her boys.

Jim was out fighting a fire when Mary went into labor. Because Mary had worked at Walton Hospital, where her baby was to be born, the staff snuck Jim in after hours to see his son. On first glance, Jim thought Paul looked like "a horrible piece of red meat." "But," he noted later, "he turned out to be a lovely baby in the end." Soon people could see Paul was going to look a lot like his dad, with the same arched eyebrows, puppy-dog brown eyes, and full, sweet lips. And he was a charmer like his dad was, too. Jim was the kind of man who would greet strangers like they were old friends.

But as much as people liked Jim, it was hard for him to make a decent living. Even after the war ended in 1945, and jobs once more became available in the cotton industry, he couldn't find one that paid much. Mary made a little more than Jim did as a nurse, but the McCartneys' small income meant housing continued to be a problem—the family moved seven times while Paul was growing up.

Yet every move they made was a bit of a step up. Paul said, looking back, "My mother was always on the lookout for a better place to live." The last couple of moves required, as Paul put it, going out to "the sticks of Liverpool," which his parents didn't mind because Mary's nursing jobs—first as a midwife, delivering babies, and later as a visiting nurse, providing home care—came with housing. "She always wanted to move us out of rough areas," Paul remembered.

With the housing crisis still acute after the war, local governments all over England were establishing "council estates," which sounds fancy but primarily meant that rural areas were being built up into planned communities. These had pluses and minuses. The estates did have their own

Visiting nurses making their rounds on bicycles were an important part of the British health system.

schools and parks but not much else. Sometimes the quickly built housing was shoddy, and the residents complained about a lack of community spirit, as well as the difficulty of getting around without much public transportation. Not many people after the war had their own cars.

The first house Paul remembered was 72 Western Avenue in the Speke community. He was only four, but he had clear memories of his house being at the very end of the inhabited area, right where the road stopped. Next to his house was an empty field. As Paul recalled, "The city always ran out where we lived." That was true again at their next move, 12 Ardwick Road in Speke. "It was really unfinished. We were slopping through mud for a year so . . . it was always this pioneering thing, we were always on the edge of the world."

Young Paul and Michael on a family trip to the Welsh countryside.

Being on the edge of the world meant there were lots of places for Paul, eight, and Michael, six, to explore. In the heavily bombarded city center, some children still played in rubble, occasionally coming across an unexploded bomb! Speke was practically country, a whole new world.

"If you went about a mile from where we lived, you would suddenly be in rural Lancashire, and it was as if you'd fallen off the end of the earth. It was all weeds and streams and fields of corn waving—everything you loved about the countryside," Paul remembered.

Young Paul would head outside with *The Observer Book of Birds,* a paperback small enough to keep in his pocket. He would pull it out and compare the photographs of birds to those flying by or perched on branches, everything from chatty magpies and singing skylarks to common blackbirds and starlings.

Sometimes, he'd follow a path that, decades before the Harry Potter books were written, had the Potterish name of Dungeon Lane. The lane meandered through fields to the banks of the River Mersey, a waterway that flows into the Irish Sea and is a dominant feature of the greater Liverpool landscape. When he was old enough to ride a bike, Paul would cycle the two and half miles to a lighthouse, where, on a clear day, he could stand on the rocky beach and see all the way to Wales.

"This is where my love of the country came from," Paul said years later. He enjoyed being a Boy Scout and racking up badges to show his proficiency in skills like knot tying and fire building. He remembered climbing trees to observe the goings-on from that heightened advantage. Even though the war was over, young men in England were still required to go into the armed services when they left secondary school. So Paul pretended he was a spy when he was up in the treetops, and in the woods he played soldier with both enthusiasm and fear as he thought about having to go into the army for real.

His obsession with joining the military also led him into the gruesome activity of killing frogs. "I had to be prepared . . . So when I got into the woods, I thought I'd better get some practice in. So I thought, frogs. That'll do . . . I thought [I'd do] a straightforward killing with a bash."

Oddly, considering England was less than a decade away from winning its own major war, Paul hid in the woods and pretended he was a Union soldier in the American Civil War. "I used to call [the frogs] Johnny Rebs; these were the rebels from the Civil War . . . I remember taking my brother down there once. He was completely horrified."

Paul also had other, smellier encounters with the natural world, thanks to his dad. Jim was an avid gardener and liked to beautify the small yards of his council houses with snapdragons and lavender. But to grow good

Paul, about age seven.

flowers, you needed good fertilizer, and the best fertilizer was horse manure. Horses were still relatively common in the area, and it was Paul and Michael's job to find whatever the local horses dropped, shovel it up, and bring it home. The most important part of the job, at least in Paul's eyes, was making sure none of his friends saw him in the process.

When Paul was nine years old, his experience with fertilizer took on a more businesslike aspect. Jim was the head of the local horticulture club and was always looking for new members. He'd send Paul out to knock on doors and drum up business. He became, he said, "virtually a door-to-door salesman . . . We used to go, 'knock, knock, would you like to join the gardening club?'" The wary neighbors would respond, "What's in it for me? Why should I?" Paul would tell them, "Well, there's free manure and you get seeds at a discount."

Besides helping his dad and giving away free manure, there was something else in it for Paul: he became more sure of himself. He later admitted he was grateful to his father for these experiences, even though he didn't always love them at the time. "I was not shy with people. I think because of all these activities my dad encouraged us into. I think it's probably very good for your confidence with people. It was all right. That was my upbringing."

There was another thing Jim encouraged his son to take part in, and that was music. Their home, no matter the location, was a place where the McCartney clan gathered, and they were a musical lot. Paul recalled a boyhood that was filled with singing. "There was quite a musical atmosphere in the house . . . The thing was, every new year, there a was always a do, a big family do. There would be someone on the piano, and most of the time that was my dad . . . he'd play old favorites, and I remember everyone joining in . . . They'd go on for hours . . . It was a fabulous musical atmosphere."

Jim, despite the success of Jim Mac's Jazz Band, always felt bad he didn't have proper musical training. So he arranged for a local woman to come to the house and give Paul and Michael lessons. Paul wanted to play piano, but he didn't want to learn scales and spend time practicing songs he didn't want to play. And he certainly didn't want to be doing any of this when he could hear the other kids playing outside.

Jim later conceded he had made a mistake starting the boys' lessons in summer, and he was disappointed that Paul quit the piano in short order. But that didn't mean Paul's interest in music stopped. Music fascinated him. It was in his bones.

"Learn to play an instrument," Jim advised Paul, "and you'll always be invited to the party."

That turned out to be very good advice.

Penny Lane

THERE WAS AN image of his mother, Mary, that always stuck in Paul McCartney's mind.

As a midwife, it was her job to be prepared, ready to leave home no matter the hour, no matter the weather to deliver a baby. When a call came saying there was woman on the council estate in labor, she would get dressed and quickly check the contents of her black medical bag, making sure she had her instruments and medications. Then, she would strap the case onto her bicycle and check the bike's lights as well as a headlamp she wore when she rode to make sure they were working properly.

"I have a crystal-clear memory of one snow-laden night when I was young," Paul recalled. "The streets were thick with snow, it was about three in the morning, and she got up and went out on her bike with the little brown wicker basket on the front, into the dark just with her little light, in her navy blue uniform and hat, cycling off down the estate to deliver a baby somewhere."

Paul sometimes thought she looked like an angel. He was also aware that his mother's career gave them a special place in the neighborhood. People would come to the door, seeking her advice or leaving her small gifts, like a little ceramic dog, a knickknack that was one of Paul's earliest memories. "It was out of gratitude [for delivering a baby]. People were always giving her presents like that."

The respect that was given to Mary because of her profession played into the larger plans she had for her boys. She saw great potential in both Paul and Michael, and she wanted them to rise above England's class system. The wealthy and powerful elites, sometimes connected to royalty, often inherited their position and money. The middle class consisted of professionals, managers, educators, successful business owners, and merchants. The working class was mostly everyone else, from plumbers and bus drivers to street sweepers, store employees, and dock and factory workers.

People in England were often defined by the way they spoke, an easy way to notice in which class you sat. As an adult, Paul talked about the differences in the way the English upper class—the posh people—would use vocabulary and phrasing compared to those on lower rungs of the social ladder. He gave an example of what each group, starting with the common folk, would say to someone who helped during an illness: "'That was nice of you. I wasn't feeling too good . . .' They [the elite] might say, 'How kind of you to think of me when I was out of sorts.'"

It wasn't just the words that were spoken; it was the accent, too. Liverpudlians often spoke with a guttural twang called *scouse*, a name lifted from the thick stew that sailors ate. There was a rough edge to it that Mary insisted her sons try to polish. Paul usually tried to please his mom, but as he got older he could get impatient with her corrections. Once he made fun of her for her own accent. "There's one moment I've regretted all my life . . . There was one time when she said 'ask' and she pronounced it posh. And I made fun of her and it slightly embarrassed her. Years later I've never forgiven myself . . . I wish I could go back and say, 'I was only kidding, Mum.'" He added he was sure Mary hadn't taken it too seriously. Nevertheless, the memory saddened him.

As a youngster, Paul rarely made his parents angry; he wasn't one to get into a lot of trouble. When he did, it was mostly for fighting with his brother, and he knew how to talk himself out of it. Michael, on the other hand, wouldn't give in. He would take his punishment, despite Paul telling him to say he didn't do it or apologize to avoid a spanking.

Paul did admit that as child he didn't always feel as pleasant on the inside as he pretended on the outside. "I was pretty sneaky. If I ever got bashed for being bad, I used to go into their bedroom when they were out and rip the lace curtains at the bottom, just a little bit, then I'd think, 'That's got them.'"

Although spanking was a common punishment during the 1950s, it wasn't a big part of the way Jim and Mary raised their boys. Love and leading by example were the cornerstones of their child-rearing. Paul's enduring memories of his mother included lots of cuddles and kisses as well as the security that came with a mother who knew how to bandage scrapes and bring down fevers.

As for Jim, who was well into his forties when his boys were growing up, he happily eased into the role of family man. He may not have dispensed hugs and kisses as freely as his wife, but he took fatherhood seriously, always making time for his sons. His boys, in turn, adored him, and it wasn't lost on them that everyone else admired Jim McCartney, too. He was described as solid, kind, and a real gentleman. Sometimes, though,

Paul thought his father was too much of a gentleman and too insistent on passing down his polite ways to his sons. Jim was so old-school, he made the boys tip their school caps when they met a woman on the street.

In ways big and small, Jim showed his devotion. Whether it was hooking up headphones to the downstairs radio and snaking them up to his sons' bedroom so they could listen at night or scraping together money for a short vacation in the countryside, he put his family first.

Whatever he was up to—music, gardening, or solving crossword puzzles in the daily newspaper—Jim tried to get his boys involved. "He was very into crosswords," Paul remembered. He would ask the boys to help him solve clues or tell them to look up a word in the dictionary if they didn't know the meaning or how to spell it. "'Learn crosswords,' he'd say. 'They're good for your word power.'" This introduction to the beauty of language, along with the stories and poetry Mary read to her sons, were the genesis of Paul's romance with words that became so important to him later, when he started writing songs.

Another aspect of his chatty dad's talk that tickled Paul was his use of obscure—or perhaps made-up—sayings. "Put it there, if it weighs a ton," Jim would say upon shaking hands. Or if he told the boys to do something, and they whined, "Why?" he'd reply, "Because there's no hair on the seagull's chest, that's why." "It was daft," Paul said. "Surreal. Perhaps that's why I loved it."

With so much emphasis on learning and getting ahead in the world, Paul understood instinctively that he was supposed to do well in school, and he did. He started out at the local Stockton Roads Infants School, but with England having a postwar baby boom, it was soon overcrowded. So Paul and Michael were transferred to the newly built Joseph Williams Primary School, a half-hour bus ride away.

Paul—bright, pleasing, and with politeness drummed into him—was a school standout who also had a real talent for art. His teachers did note that sometimes he'd try to slide on his looks and natural charm, and one wrote in a report that Paul was "a very intelligent boy who, with a little more care and application, could easily be first."

IN THE EARLY 1950S, England still hadn't completely righted itself from all it had gone through in World War II, which had ended in 1945. The fighting was over, but the memories, hardships, and rubble still clung to the country. Everyday staples like sugar, butter, cheese, meat, and tea, as well as bigger items like automobiles, were all still rationed when Paul was a boy. Paul thought that apple slices sprinkled with sugar and a can of condensed milk, sweeter and thicker than regular milk, were wonderful treats. Decades later, he said the great dream of his childhood was to have at least two cans of condensed milk.

One bright spot in the postwar gloom had been the royal wedding of the young Princess Elizabeth to the dashing Lt. Philip Mountbatten in 1947. Elizabeth and her sister, Margaret, had grown up before the country's eyes, and they were much loved by the British public. When Elizabeth's father, King George, died in 1952, she was to take his place on the throne the following year. This would mark the first time since Queen Victoria's sixty-three-year reign, which ended with her death in 1901, that there would be a female monarch. And Elizabeth was a young one at that, ascending the throne at only twenty-seven years old. With excitement building around the coronation, those who could afford it saved their money so they could buy their first television set to watch on the big day.

The McCartney family was contending with their own excitement. Paul had written an essay about the coronation of Queen Elizabeth II and was the winner for his age group in a citywide contest.

Along with the other winners, Paul was to read his composition onstage at Picton Hall in the city center. On the day of the assembly, Paul, wearing his school uniform, and his family went into Liverpool for the event. For the first time in his life, Paul says, he was really nervous. He vividly remembered that when he was called to the stage by a dignitary in a pin-striped suit, "my knees went rubbery." He added, "I was shaking like jelly." But Paul's way with words was evident; he began his composition on an exciting note with the bloody coronation of William the Conqueror in 1066, then quickly moved into the anticipation surrounding the coronation of the beloved Elizabeth. His prize was a souvenir booklet about the coronation as well as a gift certificate to a local bookstore. Paul used the certificate to buy an art book that introduced him to modern artists like Salvador Dali and Pablo Picasso and became a prized possession. As an adult, Paul was sure his winning composition was long-lost, so he was thrilled when a biographer dug it up out of the city archives.

The prize-winning composition by ten-year-old Paul was found at Liverpool's Central Library in 2009.

The British school system was an important element that bolstered England's classist society. Thanks to those difficult eleven-plus exams, only students scoring highly were going on to good schools. There wasn't much incentive to continue education past the age of fifteen or sixteen. Many kids waited for the day when they could drop out and go to work.

In Paul's class of hundreds at Joseph Williams Primary, he was one of ninety students to even take the eleven-plus exams, while everyone else took more general tests. Then, to his parents' delight, he was only one of four children at the school to pass, ensuring him a place at one of the best schools in all of England, the Liverpool Institute.

The Liverpool Institute, known to the locals affectionately as the "Inny," was a large, imposing stone edifice, built in the 1800s. Located on Mount Street, it looked down on the busy center of Liverpool. Like Quarry Bank, the Liverpool Institute was a boys' school; most schools for older kids were divided by sex. Paul, dressed in the school uniform of short gray pants, a green-and-black tie, and a cap, must have been feeling quite small when, on September 5, 1953, he walked through the massive columns that flanked the wrought iron entrance.

It wasn't just the size of the school that was intimidating. Equally impressive were the teachers, who, as at Quarry Bank, swept through the hallways in their dark gowns, similar to those worn by the professors at prestigious colleges like Oxford and Cambridge. Paul must have been aware that these teachers held his fate in their hands. The school faculty made it a practice to keep tabs on outstanding students, the ones who could be put on a path to the best colleges. After all, the school's Latin motto translated to "You were born not for yourself but for the whole world." Little did the faculty know how true this would turn out to be for Paul McCartney.

School, however, was not always easy for Paul. For one thing, it brought teasing from the kids on Speke estate. Going to the Inny set him apart from those stuck in ordinary schools, and Paul hated the way they nicknamed him "the college pudding." And unlike at primary school, where Paul shone, all of the Inny boys were good students. Paul started out pretty well in a program that concentrated on languages, but after the first year or so, his grades began slipping. What he enjoyed most in school were classes that were not essential for his class standings—art and woodworking, both of which he discovered he had a real talent for.

As for the standard curriculum, Paul consistently did well in English literature and composition. Paul was particularly inspired by one teacher, Alan Durband, known affectionately around school as Dusty. Part of his curriculum was teaching *The Canterbury Tales* by Geoffrey Chaucer. The stories were written in Old English, which was difficult to read and understand, not exactly the kind of book boys would pick up willingly. The stories were, however, full of naughty passages with sexual allusions. Knowing his young male audience, Durband introduced those first, catching his students' interest. "Then, we got interested in the other bits, too," Paul remembered admiringly, "so he was a clever bloke."

It was also in Durband's classes that Paul came face-to-face with the great Shakespeare characters Hamlet, Macbeth, and King Lear. Durband distilled the drama by focusing on the essence of each play, paring it down to a few key themes. Later, Paul would find this stripping away a useful trick when it came to writing song lyrics that had to pack story and emotion into a few lines.

At the Inny, Paul acquired a nickname, Macca, and also made two friends who would become very important to him. One was Ivan Vaughn, John's bright neighborhood friend, who also had a nickname, Ivy. The other was a younger student, who came to school a year after Paul. His name was George Harrison. George's family lived in Speke, too, and once George started at the Inny, they were often on the same half-hour bus ride to school. The boys soon found out they were both interested in music, and even though George was younger than Paul and his other friends, this shared bond would only grow stronger.

Paul was always a cute kid, but as he grew older and taller he became a handsome young man who had the girls swooning. One of the girls from the neighborhood recalled she and some of her friends had crushes on Paul. "He had this angelic-type face and we'd see it peering out from the top deck of the eighty-six bus as it passed when he was on his way to Liverpool Institute." Waiting for their own buses, they would "jump up and down and wave and shout at him." A precursor of things to come.

Now that he was a young teenager, Paul's interest in girls was growing, but since the Liverpool Institute was an all-male school, he didn't have lots of opportunities to meet them. He wished he could, though. Most of Paul's knowledge about sex came from his mother's medical books; his father was too uncomfortable with the subject to talk much about it. Paul once used his artistic talent in pursuit of this newfound interest in sex. He drew a picture that just seemed like a woman's head and legs, but when the paper was unfolded, it showed her naked body. His classmates thought it was hysterical, and Paul did, too, until Mary found the picture in his shirt pocket when she was sorting laundry. Mortified, Paul denied he had drawn it, and continued denying it for a couple of days, until finally he buckled and told the truth, much to his parents' dismay and his total embarrassment.

In 1955, when Paul was thirteen, the McCartney family made their last and most impressive move upward. Speke, as it became more developed, also became a rougher community. Mary, who had left the stressful job of midwife to become a visiting nurse, was once again on the lookout for a

Paul McCartney's home at 20 Forthlin Road.

new home. Because of her job, and through her connections with the local housing authorities, she was able to secure a house at 20 Forthlin Road in the Allerton section of Liverpool, a middle-class enclave a couple of miles from where John Lennon lived.

The simple row houses were well designed and appointed. The housing council wanted the new dwellings to fit into the neighborhood, so they added nice touches, like ebony doorknobs, a small stained glass window in each front door, and a pretty lavender hedge bordering each postage-stamp front lawn (Jim would use the lavender to make a potpourri, hoping the fragrance would cover up the smell of his pipe smoke, which Mary disliked).

The living room of Paul's house. The wallpaper was picked out by Paul and Michael.

Inside, the downstairs rooms—living room with a coal fireplace and windows looking out to the yard, dining room, and kitchen—were small, but the circular flow of the house, leading from one room to the next, made it feel more spacious.

The McCartneys added their own touches to their living room. Paul and Michael were allowed to pick out the wallpaper, but instead of choosing just one design, they chose a plain broken stripe for one wall, a blue Chinese motif for another, and a stonework design paper for the third. Placed against one wall was the upright piano, which took up a sizable space but made up for it in the pleasure it produced.

Upstairs, there was a bedroom for Jim and Mary and one for each boy. There were even a couple of luxuries: a clothes washer in the kitchen (though no dryer) and, best of all, an indoor toilet. Even though their two previous council houses were newly built, the toilet facilities had still been located outside, which was surprisingly common in 1950s England. What a relief not to have to run outside on shivery winter nights!

One of the unexpected perks of the house was that Michael's bedroom looked out on the grounds of the Liverpool Mounted Police's training center. To the brothers' delight, that meant seeing the horses go through their paces, either watching from the window or sitting outside. Once a year, there was a community show held on the grounds, sometimes hosted by a celebrity. "We used to sit on the concrete shed in the backyard and watch the police show every year for free." Paul particularly remembered the year a pretty starlet named Jackie Collins, later to become a famous author, opened the show.

The new neighborhood was close to the shopping area and bus hub Penny Lane. It was a place the McCartney boys often went to catch buses into the city and to visit friends, as well as to school. (Michael had also been accepted at the Inny by this time.) Public transit could take Paul away from his parents' prying eyes, and he had a bit of a love affair with the bright-red double-decker buses that lumbered around Liverpool. All the kids liked to climb to the top, where they were out of sight of the conductor, free to horse around and pull pranks. But Paul also enjoyed sitting up there looking out of a rain-splashed window. It gave him time to dream a little. After he was famous, Paul asked his Beatle bandmate George Harrison if he didn't miss riding around in Liverpool buses. George didn't see the romance of it, but then again, his father was a bus driver.

One of Paul's best-known Beatles songs is "Penny Lane"; he wrote it as something of a companion to John's song "Strawberry Fields Forever." Calling on his many memories about the area, Paul took visual images like the bus shelter roundabout, a barber shop, and a nearby fire station and mixed them up with people busily going about their business—a banker, a barber, and a nurse, like his mother—all under "blue suburban skies."

The Penny Lane roundabout, where both John and Paul caught buses to take them to places in and around Liverpool.

"There was a barber shop called Bioletti's," Paul later said, remembering one of his inspirations, "with headshots of the haircuts you can have in the window, and I just took it all and arted it up a little bit to make it sound like he was having a picture exhibition in his window."

It was in the house on Forthlin Road that Paul's personal musical journey began. On his fourteenth birthday, he was given a trumpet. Playing brass instruments ran in the family. His grandfather Joe McCartney had played a tuba in a brass band, and as boy, Paul had gone to listen to brass band concerts in a local park. Jim played the trumpet, as well as the piano, and his brother played the trombone. Paul had nothing against the trumpet, but he wasn't very excited about it either. As instruments go, it seemed a bit boring, and besides, Paul, who had been a choir boy at a local church, liked to sing. There was no singing while playing the trumpet.

What he *was* excited about was the guitar. British teens were just starting to hear American rock and roll, and a guitar twang got many of them going. Paul was entranced. With Jim's permission, he went to Rushworth and Dreaper's music store and traded his trumpet for a Zenith guitar. The brown-and-tan instrument wasn't much to look at and the sound wasn't great, but none of that mattered to Paul. He was determined to master the guitar.

That turned out be difficult. "[I] couldn't figure out at all how to play it. I didn't realize that it was because I was left-handed." It wasn't until he saw a picture of Slim Whitman, another lefty musician, that he realized that he had the guitar "the wrong way round." Next he had to learn to restring the guitar, no mean trick. Once that was finally accomplished, things got easier.

Just when life seemed to be settling in nicely for the McCartney family, tragedy struck.

Mary had not been feeling well for a while. She was exhausted and suffered with pains in the chest that she hoped would turn out to be indigestion. It's unclear when she received the devastating diagnosis of breast cancer. One relative said Mary knew for at least a year before she went into the hospital. Other reports say her intense pain came suddenly. In any case, in the 1950s, there was no real treatment for cancer. Whenever she received her diagnosis, Mary, especially with her medical background, must have known it was a death sentence.

The doctors decided the best they could offer was a mastectomy, a surgery that removed the breast. The day before she went to the hospital, she cleaned the house, cooked some meals, and ironed her sons' clothes. A resigned Mary told her sister-in-law, "Now everything's ready for them, in case if I don't come back."

Despite saying that, Mary probably did think she'd have a little more time. The doctors felt the surgery, which took place on October 31, 1956, went according to plan, but it took more of a toll on Mary than expected. By the time Paul and Michael came to visit her that evening, she looked ravaged by the ordeal. Still, there was joking and kisses, though Paul spotted blood on the sheets, something that stuck in his mind. A few hours after her sons left, a complication of the surgery ended Mary's life. She was forty-seven years old.

Paul felt like he'd fallen down a hole without a bottom. Nothing seemed quite real. It didn't help that the usually controlled Jim was so distraught, so insistent he couldn't live without Mary, that his relatives worried he might harm himself. So Paul and Michael stayed with aunts and uncles while Jim tried to pull himself together.

"My mother's death broke my dad up. That was the worst thing for me, hearing my dad cry. I'd never heard him cry before . . . then you know something's really wrong and it shakes your faith in everything." In another slip he'd come to regret, Paul asked his newly widowed father how the family was supposed to get along without Mary's income.

In those days, there was really no grief counseling. People, even young people, were expected to get over death and get on with life. No one ever gets over losing a loved one, but life does go on. Jim, always a responsible father, brought the boys home after a few weeks and went back to work. As for Paul, he "carried on," as he put it, though he put a protective shell around himself now that he knew how painfully life could pierce you.

One cushion for Paul and Michael was their extended family. His aunts came over to cook and clean, and his aunt Jin, Jim's sister, especially knew that what the boys needed was having a motherly figure around. She'd open her arms, Paul remembered, and tell the boys to come talk about whatever was on their minds. It helped. But with his life rearranged, and Mary and her high hopes for his future gone, Paul was at loose ends. Schoolwork now seemed meaningless. Paul needed something to hold on to, something that seemed like hope. That turned out to be music.

After Mary's death, playing the guitar felt right to Paul when everything else felt wrong. Michael called his constant playing an obsession. Paul even began tinkering with writing his own songs. The very first one he wrote was called "I Lost My Little Girl." Paul thought of it as a breakup song; as an adult, he realized it was really about Mary.

The loss of his mother left a hole in Paul's heart. Guitar in hand, he began to fill it with music. Less than a year later, someone would come into Paul's life who shared his obsession and would become his partner in shaping his ambitions and dreams in new ways. Enter John Lennon.

Gotta Be
Rock-and-Roll Music

"I REMEMBER . . . the movie *Blackboard Jungle,* which is where Bill Haley performs the song 'Rock around the Clock.' And I remember it very clearly. It was the first piece of music that ever sent a tingle up my spine."

So said Paul McCartney, recalling how the hard-driving beat of a new kind of music impacted him as a young teen. Rock and roll! It was to change the lives of Paul, John Lennon, and millions of young people in the United States, England, and beyond.

Rock music began in the United States as a potent stew of other musical genres: rhythm and blues, gospel music, country music, swing, and jazz. Rock's influence went beyond just songs and singing styles, however. Rock and roll started a youthquake that shook up, well, everything, starting with music and movies, but it also transformed the way teens dressed, how

The song "Rock around the Clock," featured in *Blackboard Jungle,* was so popular, it became a movie of its own.

they wore their hair, and, most influentially, how young people saw their world in ways big and small.

How could a musical style do all that? To understand, you have to look at what came before. Up until the twentieth century, especially in the working classes and rural societies, there were adults and there were children, and often the children worked alongside their families on farms and in factories. There wasn't always time for school, and people often married much younger than they do today. For most people, in both the US and England, there was not much of a passage between youth and adulthood.

But as the twentieth century progressed, modern influences started to alter society. New child labor laws meant children could stay in school longer, giving them more opportunities to grow and learn. In the decades that followed, economic events like the Great Depression and the devastation of two world wars unsettled people's lives in numerous ways. Birth rates fell, lives were lost, and young people became a more precious commodity. That led many parents to take more of an interest in their children's future. Still, young people dressed more or less like their parents, listened to the same music as adults, and generally saw their future as a job, marriage, and raising a family. But change was brewing among kids, who took on the name *teenagers*, a term that came into vogue after the end of World War II.

Teens began to have more time to call their own. That meant they could hang with their friends, pursue their own interests, and form their own lifestyles. Soon there were types of entertainment that were directed at this brand-new audience.

For kids in England, one of the earliest of these was a British radio program called *The Goon Show*. It premiered in 1951 under its original title, *Crazy People*, and was created by a multitalented writer and come-

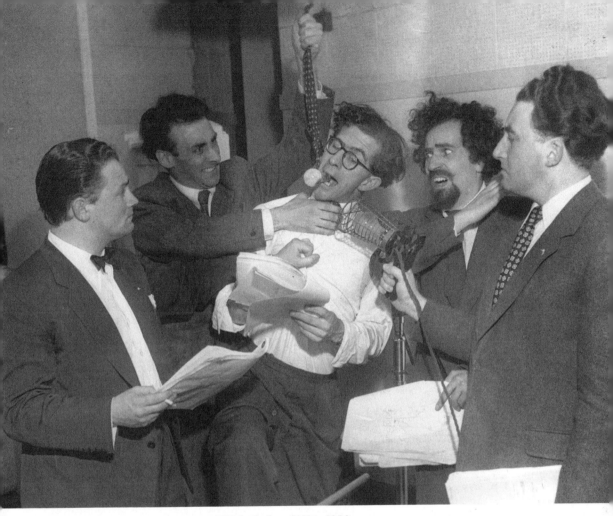

The Goon Show was broadcast on BBC Radio from 1951 to 1960.

dian, Spike Milligan. The show was a wild mix of outrageous jokes, weird sound effects, and wacky characters. The small cast, including Peter Sellers, who was to become a famous actor, made fun of everything from the British class system to politics to popular movies and books. John Lennon, in particular, was a *Goon* maniac, and when he grew up, he wrote about how important the show had been to him, noting he was only twelve when it "first hit me." John cherished the Goons because "their humor was the only proof the WORLD was insane . . . Hipper than the Hippest and madder than 'Mad,' a conspiracy against reality."

The Goon Show was in part what inspired John to write his irreverent pieces like *The Daily Howl*, and it confirmed his subversive visions. People walked through life as though it was full of logic and purpose. John suspected it was not. *The Goon Show* was a real-world confirmation that he was right, that this wasn't the case, at least not for those cool enough to see the truth.

But *The Goon Show* was just a prelude to the effect contemporary music would have on John, Paul, their friends, and the wider teen world. "Rock around the Clock" by Bill Haley and his band, the Comets, was released in 1954. By 1955, it was the number one song in the US and the UK, and it became a youth anthem in 1956 when the song was played over the credits of a movie about teenage rebellion called *Blackboard Jungle*. When an interviewer in 1981 asked John about the effect rock music had on him, he said, "I had no idea about doing music as a way of life until rock hit me." Asked specifically what hit him, John replied, "It was 'Rock around the Clock.'"

So began a whole new musical vibe, one that was exciting and hinted at endless possibilities. For most teens living in the US, it was easy to hear the new rock-and-roll sound. All you had to do was turn on the radio. But things were very different in England. There, the radio waves were owned by the government's British Broadcasting System. In the early 1950s, the popular music shows they presented stuck to songs that were strictly middle-of-road love songs, such as "Cry" by Johnnie Ray, or novelty tunes like Patti Page's "(How Much Is) That Doggie in the Window?" Kids listened in because there wasn't much else to listen to—until, a few years later, under the cover of darkness, something changed. When the sun went down on Saturdays and Sundays, Radio Luxembourg came on the air.

Luxembourg—a small country in Europe nestled between Belgium, Germany, and France—saw an opening to reach a young British audience in the mid-1950s by playing all the latest rock music from the United States. These evening shows were sponsored by record companies that would then make sure the records were available in British record stores. There was even a new modern format for the records, the 45-rpm single. Only seven inches wide, with one song on each side, they were more affordable for young people than longer record albums.

It wasn't always easy to tune in to Radio Luxembourg. The signal wasn't very strong, and persistent teens would have to fiddle with the dial to find the station, which could fade in and out. But it was worth it to hear the music play into the night. John, who now had a radio in his room, and Paul, whose dad had hooked up headphones attached to the radio downstairs, both listened avidly to Radio Luxembourg. If "Rock around the Clock" gave them a tingle, Radio Luxembourg's programming woke them, opened their eyes wide, and gave them a new vision of what the future could be. Everything about the music was fresh: the beat, the hidden sexual allusions in the lyrics, and even the names of the groups: the Platters, the Drifters, the Cadillacs.

What young British teens like John and Paul didn't know at first was the racial aspects of rock-and-roll music. Unlike in the States, there were relatively few people of African descent in England at the time, though Liverpool had more than most. Being a shipping hub, it was more cosmopolitan, a place where different kinds of people came and stayed. Before picking up other influences, the roots of rock were planted in the African American South as a more insistent form of the blues. The earliest rockers were African American musicians, like Richard Penniman, whose stage name was Little Richard. As he noted, "There wasn't nobody playing at the time but black people—myself, Fats Domino, Chuck Berry."

Because of the segregation and racial prejudice in the United States, however, it was difficult for Black artists to make money from their music. Often, songwriters would be paid a paltry sum for their songs, which would then be recorded, or "covered," by white singers, who were considered more acceptable for white audiences. Fats Domino's early rock classic "Ain't That a Shame" shot up the record charts when it was covered by the squeaky-clean white singer Pat Boone. Covers were commonplace, but as the 1950s rolled on, American disc jockeys, especially the popular Alan Freed, began promoting Black artists, who started to get the recognition they deserved.

No matter how much teens liked "Rock around the Clock," singer Bill Haley wasn't exactly the picture of youth and change. He was in his late twenties but he looked older, was slightly overweight, and was hiding a receding hairline with a spit curl in the middle of his forehead. There was a singer waiting in the wings, however, who had not just the sound but the look that kids were waiting for.

Fans admired everything about Elvis Presley, from the way he sang to the way he looked to the way he moved.

Elvis Presley burst onto the musical stage in 1954 and immediately captured the hearts of teenagers, both girls and boys. Growing up poor in Tupelo, Mississippi, Elvis soaked up (some would say appropriated) the Black musical influences surrounding him, including the gospel music he heard in church. Handsome, with a low, throaty voice, Elvis put his body into his music: strumming his guitar, swinging his hips, and literally shaking up the music scene—and, for that matter, the world. As one early rock song put it, there was a "Whole Lot of Shaking Goin' On."

"Heartbreak Hotel" was the first Elvis Presley record released in England, in the spring of 1956. Used to smooth American singers who

LEFT: Little Richard and Bill Haley pose for a publicity picture for the film *Don't Knock the Rock*.

enunciated each word, like Johnnie Ray or Frank Sinatra, John, at first, could barely make out the lyrics coming from the muttering, slurring Presley. "To us it just sounded like a noise that was *great* . . . It just broke me up. I mean, that was the end. Me whole life changed from then on . . . I thought 'This is it!'"

Paul was equally captivated by both song and singer. He had seen one of the first photos of Elvis available in England, with his long sideburns and curled lip, and thought he looked perfect. "The Messiah had arrived."

Then another musical miracle occurred a couple of months after Elvis came on the scene. A friend of John's, Michael Hill, went on holiday to Amsterdam and brought back a record of "Long Tall Sally" by the American artist Little Richard. When Michael told John he had discovered a singer better than Elvis, John said it wasn't possible. But after he and a few friends heard the song played at Hill's house, he was "stopped in his tracks."

"His reaction that day was something that stuck in everybody's memory," Hill recalled, "because he really was struck dumb by the record. He didn't know what to say, which for John was *most* unusual because he was always so good with an answer . . . I felt good because John was so hard to impress."

That moment was stuck in John's memory, too. He recalled being torn, because of his loyalty to Elvis's sound. He thought, "How could this be happening in my life? *Both* of them?" Then someone told him that Little Richard was Black. That made things easier, at least in John's mind. Since they were of two different races, they could both be his favorites. John said that at the time he didn't know one Black person in England, but his admiration for African American roots music grew and grew as he heard more of it and began understanding that almost all of rock music came from that source.

Paul was equally gobsmacked by Little Richard. The songs he heard were the first released in England in 1956: "Rip It Up" and, on the flip side, "Ready Teddy." One of Little Richard's signatures was the way he screamed during his vocals. Sometimes it sounded like a long, shrill howl— "Woooooo!" As Paul put it, "Little Richard was this voice from heaven or hell or both. This screaming voice seemed to come from the top of his head." Then Paul had a revelation. "I tried to do it one day and found I could. You had to lose every inhibition and do it." For a kid who had recently lost his mother, perhaps screaming at the top of his lungs was good therapy.

As the rock craze took hold, seemingly overnight, British boys, like their American counterparts, adopted the Elvis look. That meant a trip to the barber, where conventional schoolboy hair was turned into a DA (or duck's ass), a cut that had slicked-back sides, a pompadour in front, and a parted back coming to a point, which gave the style its name. Hair cream, and lots of it, kept the hairdo in place—and eventually led to guys who used it being called "greasers."

Both John and Paul and were among the British lads who got a DA (though not without argument from Mimi and Jim), but that was only step one. They needed the distinctive outfits that screamed they weren't wearing dad-style clothes anymore.

Even though Elvis was the catalyst for the new looks, there had been something of a clothing style revolution going on in England since the early 1950s, and it centered around young men known as Teddy Boys. The popular press portrayed these rebels against conformity as menacing, even threats to society, and sometimes they were. Their name played off the long jackets they wore, reminiscent of clothes worn in the Edwardian era, the first decade of the twentieth century. Also essential to the look were tight pants called drainpipes, or drainies, and string ties. Since American rockers wore similar looks, British teen boys began jumping on this fashion bandwagon.

Naturally, parents and teachers were not on board. Schools, at least, could enforce their rules about uniforms. Caps were required at the Inny; Paul soon found the DA and caps were not very compatible. Finally, he figured out that if he pushed his cap back on his head, the long drooping front of the hairstyle could still flop around his forehead, and the hair cream kept hat and hair stuck together. When it came to his obsession with drainies, Paul had to be devious. Jim was insistent—Paul's pants should keep their wide cuff. So, Paul went to school wearing his regulation pants, but at lunchtime, when he could, he'd nip out to a tailor and have them taken in. If Jim noticed the difference in the evening, Paul would put on an innocent expression and say, "They're the same pair you saw me go out in this morning."

His most outstanding purchase, worn only after school hours, of course, was an oatmeal-colored sports coat flecked with shiny threads. After hearing the song "A White Sport Coat (and a Pink Carnation)," he had been on the hunt for a similar look. Worn with his drainies, white shirt, and a black string tie, the jacket made Paul feel cool.

As for John, friends like Pete Shotton considered him "a fashion leader." John was the first at his school to get a DA haircut, and thanks to Julia's financial contributions, he was soon wearing tight black pants, colored jackets, and thin ties. Mimi, needless to say, was not pleased. Her worst fears about John were coming true. If his plummeting grades and disgraceful behavior weren't bad enough, now he and Pete were known as the school Teddy Boys.

In reality, though, Lotton were Teds in dress only. Real Teds could be dangerous, with brass knuckles or switchblade knives as noticeable as their string ties. As Pete recalled it, he and John moved quickly in the opposite direction if any of these rougher guys, usually in their twenties, crossed their path. "I was never really a street kid or a tough guy," John admitted. "I used to dress like a Teddy Boy and identify with Marlon Brando or Elvis Presley, but I was never really in any street fights or down-home gang . . . but a big part of one's life is to look tough."

Looking the part of rockers may have been fun for John and Paul, but when it came to the music, both boys were deadly serious. It was as if each of them—John at Quarry Bank, Paul at the Liverpool Institute—had been blundering toward a future they couldn't quite see. With the advent of rock, at last, there was light.

John's keen interest in music was not new, of course. There were his skills on the harmonica, and he carried on for a while on the accordion. Despite his mischief in church, he liked singing enough for a stint in St. Peter's choir.

On summer days as a young teen, he and Pete and their friends Ivan Vaughn, Len Garry, and Bill Turner would bike over to nearby Calderstones Park, a magnificent burst of nature that contained wooded lanes, extensive gardens, a small lake, and an ancient oak more than a thousand years old. The boys had their own spot in the park at the bottom of an incline called "the Bank" that shielded them as they talked, joked, and sometimes sang.

Len Garry liked singing and whistling, and after some coaxing, John and the others began singing, too, even if Pete worried it wasn't "manly." This was a year or so before rock hit, so the songs they sang were mostly BBC ballads, but it was clear to John's friends that, when he let himself go, he could belt out a tune. As Pete recalled, those days, "Our fifteenth birthdays were approaching. We had just discovered what girls were about, and more than anything else we had all taken an avid interest in music."

After rock and roll appeared on the scene, John desperately wanted a guitar, but he knew better than to ask Mimi to get him one. Fortunately, there was another mom he could turn to—Julia. However, Julia was reluctant to go against Mimi. They compromised by Julia teaching John the banjo at her house.

The banjo is a much simpler instrument than the guitar, and soon John had learned the basic chords that allowed him to accompany himself on songs, like Fats Domino's "Ain't That a Shame." The banjo was something, but it wasn't a guitar, and John knew how to wheedle, beg, and probably lay some guilt on Julia until she finally agreed to "lend" him some money to buy a guitar he had seen in a mail-order catalog. After John became famous, Mimi told interviewers that she had bought John his first guitar, but that pivotal purchase belonged to Julia.

It wasn't, however, much of a guitar. Piped with black-and-white trim and made of wide-grain maple—rather than the alpine spruce used in better instruments—the Gallotone Champion's proudest claim was that it was "guaranteed not to split."

Despite its flaws, for John, the guitar was a dream come true. Nevertheless, becoming a decent guitarist wasn't easy. "I think I had one lesson, but it was so much like school, I gave it up. I learnt mostly by picking up bits here and there. One of the first things I learned was 'Ain't That a Shame' and it has lots of memories for me. Then I learnt 'That'll Be the Day' . . . but I couldn't learn 'Blue Suede Shoes.'"

Paul was even more determined than John to get good at the guitar. He was helped along by a pal named Ian James. Ian owned an excellent guitar, a Rex, and he knew how to play well. He helped Paul learn more chords and play more songs, including a complicated tune called "Twenty Flight Rock," about a guy who gets out of breath climbing twenty flights up to his girlfriend's apartment. Paul was still noodling on the piano as well as playing the guitar, so his musical skills were growing by leaps and bounds.

If the effect rock and roll was having on the lads of Liverpool wasn't enough, another musical craze was sweeping across England. It was called skiffle. Like rock, skiffle's roots were American, primarily African American, mostly country blues and folk music, though the actual origins of the name *skiffle* have been lost. A British jazzman named Lonnie Donegan began playing skiffle in the mid-1950s, and the bouncy beat quickly caught on. His "Rock Island Line," an American folk song about a train coming into New Orleans, half-spoken, half-sung, was one of England's top tunes in 1956. Paul was a big fan of Donegan and went to see him when he played one of Liverpool's largest theaters, even waiting after the show was over to get Donegan's autograph. Paul never forgot how friendly and accommodating the musician was to his fans. It was a lesson Paul took to heart when he had fans of his own.

The infectious rhythms attracted aspiring musicians in England because simple instruments could make the skiffle sound. A guitar was important, but other instruments needed for skiffle could be found around the house. Everyone at the time had a tin washboard that, when strummed, made an interesting squeaky sound. You could make a bass fiddle by attaching a broom handle to a metal washtub or tea chest and adding strings. Blow into a jug for deep beats, and if a guitar was too expensive, it was possible to construct one from a wooden cigar box, stringing it up to a wooden handle.

The skiffle group Les Hobeaux performing in Hastings, England, 1957.

The skiffle craze wasn't just about listening. With instruments so accessible, skiffle bands began springing up across the country. By 1957, there were over two hundred homegrown bands in Liverpool. So it wasn't a big leap for John and his friends to figure that they should start a skiffle band, too.

Details of how the band got started have gotten fuzzy over time. One story has John getting the idea and casually asking Pete, "Why don't we start up a skiffle group, then?" Other friends claim it was their idea.

Either way, John quickly became the acknowledged leader. Band members drifted in and out, but soon a core group formed. Pete Shotton, of course, was in, even though he didn't like being onstage and had no musical talent whatsoever. John told him it didn't matter; anyone could play a washboard. So that became his "instrument." Len Garry put together a tea-chest bass to play, Rod Davis was on banjo, and Eric Griffiths, a beginner on the guitar like John, was a regular. Ivan Vaughn, more interested in his studies than music, sometimes substituted when one of the other boys wasn't available. Eric pulled off something of a coup by finding a drummer for the group. Colin Hanton was an older teen, already out of school and working as an upholstery apprentice, which gave him money to buy a small drum kit. With an actual drummer, John began to feel he had a real band.

But what to call the group? They hit on a name they thought was cool, the Blackjacks, then quickly learned there was a more established group in Liverpool with the name. Pete Shotton says he was the one who came up with the name that stuck. "Since our native Woolton was pocked with sandstone quarries and most of us also attended Quarry Bank High School, the 'Quarry Men' seemed as good a choice as any. John and I, moreover, had always been amused by a line in our school song, 'Quarry Men, strong before our birth.'"

Though it was supposed to be a skiffle band, John was insistent that the Quarry Men also play other kinds of music, especially, of course, rock and roll. The boys got off to an enthusiastic start. The first order of business was finding places to practice. They began meeting in Pete Shotton's backyard, in a dilapidated corrugated-iron bomb shelter left over from the war, and Mimi would sometimes allow them to practice in the side yard at Mendips, but the noise tended to bother her student boarders. Neither spot could protect from the cold or rain. So, often the practice sessions would move indoors to Julia's house on Bloomfield Road.

Practicing at Julia's was great. There were no worries about "minding their manners." Here was a place where they could laugh, sing, strum, smoke, and even swear. Julia herself was a revelation; there was nothing "mum-like" about her. Not only was she happy to welcome them, she was a cheerleader, and when the boys took a break, they could listen to the stack of records she collected. "We discovered Gene Vincent there," Eric Griffths recalled. Julia had a copy of Vincent's "Be-Bop-A-Lula," which John and the band went wild over. They played it so often that even the affable Julia asked them to stop.

"Julia was unlike anyone I'd ever met before," said one of John's mates. Drummer Colin Hanton recalled the time that the band was practicing at Mimi's and John was having trouble figuring out some chords. "So it was off to his mum's. Julia immediately got out the banjo and showed him everything he needed to know. If one of the riffs got too complicated, she'd sing things to emphasize what she was trying to explain. I thought, 'Crikey, this is his *mother.* They're talking about *music*!' It was a lot for a lad like me to digest."

There had never really been any doubt that John was the leader of the band, but even some of its members were surprised by just how comfortable he was as a lead singer and how dedicated he was to keeping the Quarry Men going. He may not have put any effort into his schoolwork, but he was just the opposite when it came to music. He was particularly insistent that the boys were learning new music, even if they couldn't always master the chords or learn the correct words to songs (lyrics were often scribbled on scraps of paper as they listened to music on Radio Luxembourg or heard records played in music store listening booths).

John's command of how a band should operate was also something to behold. Nigel Walley, John's childhood friend and neighbor, was amazed at how John seemed to know just what to do to keep things moving. "It was right there at his fingertips. It wasn't this concept he'd worked out; it came naturally to him. The amazing thing, too, was how effortlessly he got everyone else to follow him."

Nigel was such a poor musician, the Quarry Men didn't want him onstage, even playing the washboard. But Nigel did want to be a part of the group, so he volunteered to be the band's manager. To be clear, no one was clamoring to hire the fledgling band. That didn't stop the optimistic Nigel from having cards printed up.

COUNTRY. WESTERN. ROCK 'N' ROLL. SKIFFLE

THE QUARRY MEN

OPEN FOR ENGAGEMENTS

7

Come Together

"THE GUITAR'S ALL very well, John, but you'll never make a living out of it!"

So said Mimi, and she said it so often that when John became famous, he gave her a plaque with the words engraved on it. She hung it on the wall of the charming ivy-covered cottage by the sea that he was able to buy for her—with money he made playing a guitar.

In 1957, though, Mimi was right. John was making plenty of music but almost no money. And worse, this was John's last year of school at Quarry Bank. If he failed his O-level tests, the ones that would decide if he'd continue on with his education, his future seemed dim. There was one bright spot. A stint in the National Service was no longer in his future. The age limit had first been raised, and then the military obligation to serve had been eliminated. John, Paul, and many young men in their age group breathed a sigh of relief. Their futures were their own now.

What was uncertain, at least for John, was how that future would play out.

He did know he wanted it to revolve around music. For a while, his only other thought had been that he'd be an artist. Art seemed a tenuous way to support himself, and John's vague, half-joking plan was to find a patron who would support him. He talked about this in an interview he gave after the success of the Beatles. "I was always thinking I was going to be a famous artist and possibly I'd have to marry a very rich old lady, or man, to look after me while I did my art. But then rock 'n' roll came along, and I thought, 'Aha-ha, this is the one.' So I didn't have to marry anyone or live with them."

As for Paul, at the start of 1957, he was still trying to come to terms with his mother's death and the family's new living arrangements. Even with his aunts' help, more responsibility fell to Paul. Michael was at the Inny now, so Paul had to look out for his younger brother. He also had to take on some of the cooking, so there would be a hot meal ready for Jim when he got home. "I learned to cook some things. I used to take a tin of tomatoes and boil them down to make a very good tomato puree." He also prided himself on his mashed potatoes, though he had to admit that pretty much anyone could mash potatoes.

Unlike John, Paul wasn't really thinking about a career in music. Even though his grades continued to slide after his mother's death, they were good enough to get him training as a teacher. Maybe not a college professor as his mother had hoped, but the standards weren't as high for teachers at lower schools. It was music, though, that occupied most of his thoughts. Michael remembered, "The minute he got the guitar, that was the end. He played it on the lavatory, in the bath, everywhere." Especially the lavatory, because Paul quickly learned the small area with a toilet to sit on had the best acoustics in the house.

Paul and his pal Ian James continued to practice together. Sometimes, in an effort to pick up girls, they'd go to local fairs and amusement parks with their guitars slung around their shoulders. "We used to go around everywhere together dressed the same and think we were really flash." Paul figured being a musician would only increase his standing with the "birds," as girls were nicknamed in England.

John, too, was beginning to see that music was a lure for girls—at a local street fair, girls in the audience tried to pull him down from the back of the lorry that the band was using as a stage. But female fans were just a side benefit. Much more important was making sure the Quarry Men kept improving. John felt performing before an audience was the key to making the group really step up its game. Although most of the gigs the Quarry Men played were nonpaying—a party here, a school dance there—Nigel Walley was determined to pump up the band's reputation. There were a couple of memorable jobs for the Quarry Men that helped give them more confidence in the late winter and spring of 1957 when John was sixteen.

The first came through a connection Nigel had made while caddying at the Lee Park Golf Club. Lee Park had been formed by a group of Jewish families who had been denied membership to other Liverpool golf clubs because of their religion. One of the members, Dr. Joseph Sytner, was looking for a band to play at a club social event. Nigel told him he managed a skiffle group and that they would be happy to play, even after Dr. Sytner told him that there wouldn't be any payment.

There were two reasons Nigel agreed. For one, performing for a large crowd in a formal setting would be something the Quarry Men had never done before, and Nigel knew the group could use the experience. But perhaps more importantly, Nigel was aware that Dr. Sytner's son, Alan, owned a hip venue in the center of Liverpool called the Cavern Club. The Cavern, a jazz club, was patterned after the dark, smoky clubs Alan had visited in Paris. Jazz was really the only kind of music he liked—he detested rock and roll. But with a nod to skiffle's popularity, he hired skiffle bands to play between sets or when the jazz musicians took their breaks. A gig at the Cavern would be a feather in the caps of the Quarry Men, and Dr. Sytner agreed that if the group did well at his event, he would put in a word for them with Alan.

The night of the event, John was nervous but thrilled as well. Pete Shotton said, "John reacted as though we were playing the Palladium [London's biggest theater]." John decided that in a nod to the upscale occasion, the band should dress a little better than they usually did, so white shirts and black jeans were chosen to give them a more cohesive look. As for the program, skiffle music would be played as promised, but John told the band they'd play a little rock as well.

The venue, the country club's lounge, had been set up with chairs, but the boys were surprised when the well-dressed crowd filed in after dinner and there were more than double the thirty or so attendees they had expected. There was even a microphone and speakers set up, to John's delight. This was the first time they had ever gotten to play with professional equipment.

Nigel remembered the event as an unqualified success. The Quarry Men rose to the occasion and played better than they ever had. The crowd clapped and sang along and laughed when John made jokes between songs. Nigel was astounded at how well John handled the crowd of adults. "John was very witty that night, throwing off one-liners and quips. In between numbers, he came out with the funniest lines. Someone in the crowd would say something, and John would twist it into something else. They chuckled at everything he threw at them. It was fantastic." When it was all over, even though there was to be no payment, Dr. Sytner passed a hat, and it filled up with fifteen or so pounds, more money than they had ever made before. Unsure about whether he should say something to the doctor about the Cavern Club, Nigel decided to let the band rest on its laurels, at least for the evening.

He needn't have worried. Within a few days, Alan Sytner called him and booked the band for the Cavern Club. It was only to play in the "skiffle interlude," as he called it, songs between jazz sets, but the Quarry Men felt it was an important step up.

Or, literally, a step down. The Cavern was partially underground, part of an old produce warehouse on a gloomy cobblestone street littered with garbage. To get into the club, you had to stumble down a dark staircase. Not that the tiny stage area was that much brighter, lit as it was by a single bulb hanging from the ceiling. The performance area itself was divided into three sections—the middle one had a small stage that faced fifty or so chairs. The other two areas were for dancing and mingling. The club's name came from both its close, almost claustrophobic, feeling and as homage to Le Caveau Français—the French Cave—a jazz club Alan liked in Paris.

The run-up to the band's performance was filled with nervous energy and disagreements. John wanted rock and roll in the playlist, but that seemed a bad idea to some of the other band members, who knew that jazz fans were often hostile to rock. Rod Davis, in particular, felt it was disrespectful to Alan, who had hired them, but John wouldn't back down, so Rod let it go.

The day of the show, the Quarry Men started out with a couple of traditional skiffle songs. Then, John motioned the group to segue into "Don't Be Cruel," followed by several other rock tunes. The audience looked unhappy, and Alan Sytner grew progressively angrier. A couple of songs in, he passed John a note: "Cut out the bloody rock and roll!"

After their set was over, the band was dejected, all except John. He felt he had gotten the experience he wanted while staying true to his artistic aesthetic. That was the Quarry Men's last gig at the Cavern Club for a while, though several years down the road, it would be known as Liverpool's most popular spot to see a band called the Beatles.

There was another experience in the spring of 1957 that gave John the hope that perhaps the idea of a career in music was not so far-fetched. With skiffle all the rage, skiffle contests broke out all over England. Most were small-time affairs at movie houses or fairs. One, however, had more prestige. Carroll Levis was an English celebrity who traveled the country conducting talent contests. He would then put the winners together in an all-star touring show or, for the luckiest, on his television show. TV was still new to English homes, and anyone who got to appear on the small screen could become a star. The skiffle contest was to be held at one of Liverpool's impressive movie palaces, the Empire. A win would open the door to fame and fortune, which was fast becoming John's dream. He was happy to wait in a long line to apply for a place in the show.

As they had for the country club event, the Quarry Men dressed in white shirts and black pants, and perhaps because they were intimidated by Carroll Levis, the playlist, for once, didn't include any rock songs. The Quarry Men's three-minute set onstage went surprisingly well. The only competition they had was a group from Wales who had brought a busload of fans with them. John was feeling pretty good about the Quarry Men's chances, when Levis dealt them what John felt was a low blow. The show was running a little short, so Levis had the Welsh group come back and sing another song, which gave them an advantage. The winner was to be decided by the applause of the audience. It was so close, the Quarry Men and the Welsh group tied, and Levis had to give the audience a do-over. This time, the vote was clear: the Quarry Men had lost. Fame and fortune were going to have to wait.

Life for John after the talent contest began moving in slow motion. He took his prep O-levels and flunked everything except art and English, and even in those he barely scraped by. Instead of studying more for the real exams, John decided to do nothing at all to raise his scores. So he had plenty of time on his hands, but at just that moment, the Quarry Men's performance opportunities seemed to dry up. The only thing on their schedule was the annual fête at St. Peter's Church in Woolton. It was Pete Shotton's mother who had gotten them the job. Brass bands usually provided the music at the event, but Mrs. Shotton asked the planning committee to add a skiffle band for the younger crowd. Both Pete and John had been confirmed at St. Peter's, she told them, so the Quarry Men were the obvious choice. (She didn't mention that John had bragged he'd only gone through the confirmation process because he knew he'd get gifts.)

The Quarry Men were excited about playing at the fête; here was a chance to shine in front of friends and neighbors. John took special care to look good that day. He styled his hair high into a pompadour, carefully flicking a curl down on his forehead, Elvis-style. Julia had bought him a new red-and-white-checked shirt for the occasion, which he wore with the sleeves rolled up the elbows, and his black drainies were nice and tight. John escaped the house before Mimi could call him a Teddy Boy.

The tradition of a Woolton celebration had been going on for forty years. It was a day to honor the church's namesake, St. Peter, but it was

The program handed out to visitors at the Garden Fete at St. Peter's Field, the event where John Lennon met Paul McCartney.

GARDEN FETE

ST. PETER'S CHURCH FIELD

WOOLTON PARISH CHURCH   Rector: M. Pryce Jones.

Saturday, 6th July, 1957

at 3 p.m

ADMISSION BY PROGRAMME.
CHILDREN 3d.

PROCEEDS IN AID OF CHURCH FUNDS

PROGRAMME

STALLS   —   SIDESHOWS   —   ICE CREAM   —   LEMONADE

Teas and Refreshments in large Marquee situated behind the hut.

2-00 p.m.	PROCESSION leaves Church Road, via Allerton Road, Kings Drive, Hunt's Cross Avenue; returning to the Church Field. Led by the Band of the Cheshire Yeomanry. Street Collection by the Youth Club during the procession.
3-00 p.m.	CROWNING OF THE ROSE QUEEN (Miss Sally Wright) by Mrs. THELWALL JONES
3-10 p.m.	FANCY DRESS PARADE. Class 1. Under 7 years. Class 2. 7 to 12 years. Class 3. Over 12 yearss. Entrants to report to Miss P. Fuller at the Church Hall before the procession.

3-30 p.m. to 5-00 p.m.	MUSICAL SELECTIONS by the Band of the Cheshire (Earl of Chester) Yeomanry. Band-master: H. Abraham (By permission of Lt.-Col. G.C.V. Churton, M.C., M.B.E.).
4-15 p.m.	THE QUARRY MEN SKIFFLE GROUP.
5-15 p.m.	DISPLAY by the City of Liverpool Police Dogs. By kind permission of the Chief Constable and Watch Committee.
5-45 p.m.	THE QUARRY MEN SKIFFLE GROUP.

8-0p.m.   GRAND DANCE in the CHURCH HALL

GEORGE EDWARDS BAND *also The Quarry Men Skiffle Group*

TICKETS 2/-
REFRESHMENTS AT MODERATE PRICES

also a fundraiser. As the homemade floats waited to snake around the streets of Woolton, scouts and young churchgoers collected money from the folks chattering and waiting for the festivities to begin. At two o'clock, the Rose Queen, Sally Wright, decked out in a summery silk dress, was sitting astride the first float behind a brass band, twenty strong, which led the march to the church. Next came the floats, decorated with colorful bunting. They represented various local organizations and were piled with excited Woolton children, waving to the crowd. Finally, on King Street, the Quarry Men scrambled on the last flatbed truck in the parade line. The boys were supposed to be playing as their truck drove along, but after swaying and stumbling on the moving vehicle, they sat down and waved

to the bystanders. Colin hit a rim shot on his drum once in a while, and Rod, on the banjo, picked out a few tunes, just to make it look they were providing something in the way of music.

Their lorry pulled into the open field behind the church, where all kinds of stalls were set up, some selling treats like ice cream or lemonade, others for games. The Quarry Men were scheduled to play at 4:15, so they had time to wander around before they had to set up on the makeshift stage. Finally, it was time to haul their gear onstage, including Colin's drum kit, with the name Quarry Men painted neatly on the bass drum. Then, it was showtime!

They kicked off with the song "Maggie May." Playing before a sizable, happy crowd upped John's performance. He was delighted to see Julia and his little sisters, Julia and Jackie, in the audience. Mimi showed up, too, and even she seemed pleased by the audience's response to the band.

The day was turning hot and humid, but that hadn't stopped Paul McCartney from wearing his light-colored jacket with the shiny threads to the fête. It wasn't a long bike ride from Allerton to Woolton, but it was a sweaty one. The Quarry Men had already started playing their set by the time Paul arrived and pushed his way toward the front of the crowd.

The first thing he noticed was John Lennon belting out the Del-Vikings song "Come Go with Me"—with the wrong lyrics.

"Well, I love, love you, darling, come and go with me / down, down, down to the penitentiary."

Penitentiary? The real words, Paul knew, were "Come home with me / way beyond the sea."

The Quarry Men strumming on their way to the fête.

John Lennon on the day of the fête. Pete Shotton is behind him. Somewhere in the audience is Paul McCartney.

John was always struggling to write down the correct lyrics he strained to hear over Radio Luxembourg or as he listened to records played in music shops. When he couldn't quite decipher his scribblings, he'd make things up. Even before their introduction, Paul was getting a look at John's imagination and delight in wordplay.

That John was singing the Del-Vikings song was another insight into him for Paul—how devoted John was to rock. Rock lovers would, of course, be familiar with the music of Elvis, or even Little Richard. "Come Go with Me," barely available in England, was not on most fans' radar. It was a favorite of Paul's, though, and apparently of John's.

There was one thing that Paul couldn't figure out about John's playing, however. He didn't seem to be playing chords in any way that looked familiar to Paul. Eric, the other guitarist, was just strumming along, and while John was actually picking out chords, he wasn't using all the strings. Looking more closely, Paul realized that was because John was only playing banjo chords.

Ivan Vaughn, looking forward to introducing John and Paul, met up with Paul by the time the set was over. The Quarry Men jumped off the stage and headed over to a tent where the performers could hang out. Ivan and Paul followed, sidestepping the next entertainment act: police dogs doing tricks.

Inside the tent, Ivan introduced Paul to the Quarry Men. As Pete remembered it, John and Paul were a bit wary of each other. Colin put it more bluntly: "John and Paul circled each other like cats." Paul, during the performance, had recognized John as one of the Teddy-looking boys he sometimes saw around Penny Lane or riding the bus. "I saw him a few times before I met him—'Oh, he's that feller, that Ted who gets on the bus.' You notice who's hip." Realizing who John was made Paul suddenly conscious of how much younger he was than the other band members. At just fifteen, he was almost two years younger than John. "I was just on the wrong side of the cusp and they were just on the right side of it. That's how I remember feeling."

But the difference in their ages melted away after Paul asked to play a guitar and launched into "Twenty Flight Rock." All the Quarry Men remember that moment as electric.

Once Paul got started, he didn't seem to want to stop. He played "Be-Bop-A-Lula" and did a couple of Elvis songs. The Quarry Men looked at each other. Who was this kid? "He gave a great performance," Colin had to admit. "Showing off but not in a big-headed way."

Paul and Ivan watched the Quarry Men's second set and then explored the fête. As dusk fell, they turned up at the church hall, where a dance band was to be the main attraction; the program announced the George Edwards Band would play but noted "also the Quarry Men Skiffle Group."

While waiting for the evening's dance to begin, Paul went up and began noodling on the church hall's old upright piano, launching into his Little Richard impersonation, complete with screams. Had he finally overdone it? He didn't seem worried about it, and the boys, except for the more cautious John, warmed to Paul, his confidence, and of course, his talent. By the time the fête was over and the band adjourned to a pub (hoping to be served, even though everyone but Colin was too young to legally drink), it seemed natural that Paul would join them. But would John ask him to become one of the Quarry Men?

There are conflicting stories about how Paul was actually asked to join. In the last interview John Lennon gave, he said that he asked Paul to be a member that night, but no one else remembered it that way. Eric and Rod said Paul just started coming around with his guitar. However, Paul says it was Pete Shotton who offered the invitation, and Pete's memory of the moment is clear and full of details.

After the fête and a few laughs at the pub, John and Pete had walked home together. "Well, Pete, what did you think of him . . . What would you think about having him in the group, then?"

Pete thought that would be fine, but John was in no hurry to get in touch with Paul. A couple of weeks later, Pete saw Paul riding his bike in Woolton, and they stopped and talked. After a few pleasantries, Pete plunged ahead. "I've been talking with John about it, and we thought maybe you'd like to join the group."

Paul took a moment to think it over—or pretended to—and finally agreed that, yeah, he would like to join the band, though not for a while. He was off to scout camp, and after that, he and his father and brother were going to spend a week at Butlin's Holiday Camp in York. When he got back, in August, he would join the Quarry Men.

Paul and Michael, as they usually did, spent a week at a scout camp, this year in Derbyshire. Then they were going on a bittersweet vacation with their father, something they had always done before with Mary. Butlin's was a chain of camps that were meant to provide affordable vacations for British families. Each facility had a pool, places to eat, games, and activities, including talent shows. One of those shows was the venue for Paul McCartney's first appearance onstage. A member of his large extended family worked at the camp and made sure that Paul and Michael got a place in the show. Michael had broken his arm at scout camp and didn't want to perform wearing a cast, but Paul insisted, eager to sing "Bye Bye Love," an Everly Brothers song with sweet harmonies, recorded by the country-rock duo from Iowa. Calling themselves the McCartney Brothers, they did the tune, and then to Michael's annoyance—after finally overcoming his embarrassment to get onstage—he was practically pushed off by Paul so he could do a solo Little Richard tune.

John's summer was not nearly as pleasant. He got the results of his O-level tests at the end of July and learned that he had failed every subject. Despite his complete lack of preparation for the exams, John was surprised that he had not at least passed art and English as he had done in the prep tests. Whatever hopes he had for his musical future, his immediate reality was that he was finished with school, had no prospect of a job, and had no real desire to find one.

Mimi, thoroughly disgusted that John had flunked his tests, was not about to let that be the end of the story. She had put in too much time, effort, affection, and discipline into molding John to have him branded a failure. When she learned that he and Pete were toying with the idea of taking a course to become ship stewards, she saw red. John would follow in Alf Lennon's footsteps over her dead body. She marched over to Quarry Bank and confronted the headmaster, Mr. Pobjoy. What did he intend to do for John? Mr. Pobjoy protested that John's future wasn't his problem. Mimi begged to differ. The school had six years to shape the boy, and in her opinion, it was the school that had failed John, not the other way around.

No doubt Mimi knew that the school had tried its best with a student who had done all he could to laugh off his studies and the school's social norms, but, as she did with many people, a determined Mimi struck fear into Mr. Pobjoy. He had only been at Quarry Bank a year, and though he had had run-ins with John and Pete, he thought it wouldn't hurt to fix things up if he could. He decided to check with the rest of the faculty to see if someone could help solve the problem of John Lennon's future.

One teacher did have an idea. He had been exasperated by John like everyone else but thought he showed artistic talent. The teacher had even shown one of the confiscated *Daily Howl* editions to a friend who taught at the Liverpool College of Art, and she had agreed that there was an originality and cleverness to John's efforts. So the three of them made some calls, pulled a few strings, and, perhaps even to their own surprise, secured John a place at the art school.

John wasn't one to show people how appreciative he was of their efforts on his behalf, but in this case, he was grateful. He knew he had been saved from an uncertain fate, and by attending art college, he could continue on as he had been: doing as little as possible at school and concentrating on his music.

The other big interest in John's life was girls. John, as well as being the leader of his gang when he was younger, also seemed to know more about sex than the other boys. However, the information he passed on

John's artwork was unusual and amusing enough to get him into art school.

often came from dirty jokes, so it was not close to being accurate. By the time of the Woolton fête, John's unconventional good looks and cheeky attitude were a magnet for girls, who now included fans of the Quarry Men. John liked their attention very much, but he also had a steady girlfriend who either didn't know about the other girls or ignored the fact of them. Barbara Baker was a neighborhood girl who'd grown up to be a gorgeous teenager. Her initials were even *B. B.*, like John's fantasy girl, the French actress Brigitte Bardot.

They had only seen each other in passing over the years, but one day Barbara and a friend encountered John and Len, the Quarry Men's bass player, in Calderstones Park. Barbara and Len paired off at first, but after a couple of weeks, John stepped in and told Barbara that they should be a couple. The romance, which lasted more than a year, was hot and heavy. Since there was hardly anywhere they could have privacy, they often spent summer evenings making out in the graveyard adjacent to St. Peter's Church. One of the gravestones belonged to a woman named Eleanor Rigby. A song titled with her name became a Beatles hit almost a decade later.

John, taking his cue from the males around him, didn't see young women as equals, but he did have a romantic side. "He wrote pages and pages of poetry to me," Barbara recalled. "'Here,' he would say, 'I've written you a poem. Read it!'"

Because Barbara lived in the neighborhood and had known John forever, Mimi was willing to have her around, but like all John's friends, Barbara thought it was more fun to go to Julia's, where she got a warmer welcome.

As the summer of 1957 drifted into autumn, John, facing his seventeenth birthday, must have felt like he was at a crossroads. His old friends were drifting away, some to continue their studies, others to get jobs. Even the Quarry Men were starting to crack apart. Rod Davis, the banjo player, never made a comeback with John after voicing his opinion about not playing rock at the Cavern Club, and he decided he was ready to move on. Len Garry, an excellent student, knew it was time to buckle down and had less time for the band. Then there was Pete. Pete, like John, had failed all his O-level tests. He shocked his friends—and, for that matter, himself—when he decided his next step would be to sign up for the cadet program at the police academy. He couldn't quite explain his motivations, other than to say the shiny brochure put out by the academy made police work look like fun. Maybe he wondered what it would be like to stop troublemakers instead of being one. "Kids of John's and my generation still cherished the traditional image of the friendly, helpful English bobby," he explained later. And Nigel Walley's father, someone Pete admired, was a policeman.

He decided to give it a go and took the course, which was held at the school behind Paul's house.

Pete, as it turned out, was more enthusiastic about becoming a police cadet than he was about staying in the band. The truth was, though he liked having fun with his mates, he still hated being onstage. Nerves always kicked in before a show, and during the set he felt stupid since all he was doing was strumming a tin washboard. The problem was, he didn't know how to tell John he wanted out.

John and Pete may have had a million laughs over the years, but neither was the sort who would or could have an honest discussion about Pete's place in the band. It would have been too embarrassing. John, though, always sensitive to someone else's vulnerabilities, knew how self-conscious Pete was when he had to perform. As Pete tells it, in the end, John found a "neat way to get me off the hook."

The Quarry Men had just a finished a performance at a party for Colin's aunt. To the band's delight, they found that the beer was flowing, and no one was stopping teenagers from getting their share of the drink. "John and I proceeded—for the first time in our lives—to get rip-roaring drunk. (Or so we thought. I doubt we actually had more than three or four beers apiece.) Toward the end of the evening, the two of us found ourselves sitting cross-legged on the floor . . . In my inebriated condition, John seemed to be in particularly fine form as he reeled off one witticism after another. After initially reducing me to gibbering hysterics, he peremptorily seized my washboard and broke it over my head."

"Well," John said, "that takes care of that problem."

Feeling no pain thanks to the beer, a woozy, boozy Pete was both shocked and relieved to realize his days as a musician were over. As for John, Pete later noted sagely, "He was always good at making decisions."

Twelve-year-old George Harrison.

You Really Got
a Hold on Me

IF IT HADN'T been for two old wooden doors, there might never have been a musical group known as the Beatles. The first opened out of a hallway in the Liverpool Institute High School for Boys, where Paul was a student, into a small, overgrown courtyard that was bookended by a second door, which opened into the Liverpool College of Art, John's new school.

The art school had originally been a part of the Inny, but in 1883, an impressive stone building of its own was built right next door. This particular side door leading into the college wasn't used much, but for Paul it was an exciting entrance into another world. Walk down the cast-iron stairs and you were in the college cafeteria, where there were no rules, just older kids, smoking and talking while tucking in to the cheap school meals, like spaghetti on toast, that were much better than the "cabbage and boiled grasshoppers" they served at the Inny. But the cafeteria's biggest attraction for Paul, and later for his fellow student George Harrison, was that it was the place where John Lennon hung out. This close proximity allowed the younger boys to play the guitars they sometimes brought to school. If they didn't have their instruments, they would talk about music and, in general, just get closer to John, who, to them, seemed the epitome of cool.

Art college was something of a revelation for John. He wasn't expecting much, and as at Quarry Bank, he didn't put in much effort. There were required subjects, but John hadn't bothered to sign up for classes that would showcase his talents, so he was stuck in courses like lettering, which required just the kind of precision he was incapable of. "I should have been an illustrator or in the painting school, but I found myself in lettering. I didn't turn up for something, so they had just put me in that . . . They might as well have put me in skydiving for all the use I was at lettering."

John may not have liked his classes, but he did enjoy the freedom that college offered. Classes were optional, and students could work at their own pace. Still, it was hard for him to feel comfortable at first. Most of the students were "arty" in a way John wasn't. He found their conversations pretentious, their love of jazz music ludicrous, and he sneered at their herdlike choice of attire: polo shirts in warm weather, turtlenecks when it was cooler, duffle coats uniformly tan or navy, with scarves in the school colors—blue, yellow, and black—wrapped around their necks.

John marched around the campus in a large tweed overcoat belonging to his uncle George that he found hanging in a spare closet, and underneath he still wore his Teddy Boy outfits, which the other students looked at with bemused surprise. Bill Harry, who was to become a friend, had a distinct memory: "John Lennon striding around with a DA haircut, brothel creepers [crepe-soled shoes], drape jacket. It was as if a Teddy Boy had walked in off the street into this strange place where everyone else dressed the same."

John did manage to find a couple of other people at school he got close to. Bill introduced him to talented Stuart Sutcliffe, who was considered one of the best artists at the college. Jeff Mahoumand, the tall, strapping son of an Algerian father and Italian Spanish mother, was ten years older than John and had spent time in the British military, but they had interests in common, including some esoteric subjects like palm reading. As for girls, John was open to possibilities. He was intrigued by Cynthia Powell. Cynthia, who lived across the Mersey River in the upscale neighborhood of Hoylake, was prim and proper, hardly John Lennon's type. He spent the early months of their acquaintance making fun of her uptight manner, even as he endlessly borrowed pencils from her since he always forgot to bring them to their lettering class. But when he learned that Cynthia was as nearsighted as he was, they forged a friendly bond.

Even as he was finding his way at school, John was still devoting most of his time to his music. Skiffle was just about dead; rock, which had started out with just a few great sounds, was now bursting with new talent and different takes on the music. There was Carl Perkins's rockabilly "Blue Suede Shoes" (also recorded by Elvis), "Little Darlin'" by the Diamonds, Sam Cooke's "You Send Me," and "Great Balls of Fire," pounded out on the piano by Jerry Lee Lewis. Lewis's incessant beat intrigued Paul enough to put down the guitar now and then to play the piano.

The fall of 1957 saw a reboot of the Quarry Men. Pete and Rod were gone, which left John and Eric on guitar, Len thumping away on bass when not busy with school, Colin on drums, and now Paul was an additional guitarist. With a new member, practice became even more important, and the boys made the rounds of the available houses. Even though Mimi was paying John's expenses, and he still lived mostly at Mendips, he was spending more time—weekends and longer—at Julia's. Julia welcomed Paul, and, like all of John's friends, he found her amazing. Having lost his own mother, Paul was attuned to John's feelings about the unconventional relationship John had with Julia.

"For you to be a teenage boy and not living with her is very sad. It's horrible. I remember him not liking it all . . . when we left there was always a tinge of sadness about John. On the way back, I could always tell that he loved the visit and he loved her but was very sad he didn't live with her."

Julia may have been glad to have Paul around, but Mimi was not taken with him, falling for neither his sweet face nor his good manners. There seems to be no particular reason Mimi didn't like Paul, other than that he was accompanying John farther down the musical path she thought both foolish and a roadblock to a respectable future.

She either knew or figured out that John was bothered by their difference in age, so whenever Paul rang the doorbell, she would call out, "John, your little friend is here." Then she would send Paul around to the side entrance. For his part, Paul thought that Mimi didn't dislike him quite as much as she claimed to. Even as she put him down, he insisted there was a twinkle in her eye.

Mimi may have rebuffed Paul, but Jim McCartney, usually welcoming to his sons' friends, was downright scared of the influence John Lennon could exert on his son. Jim based his opinion not just on John's rough looks—though that didn't help—but on his chip-on-the-shoulder rudeness that had annoyed adults since John was a boy. More than once, Jim warned Paul, "He'll get you into trouble, son."

If his father was worried about John, Paul's brother Michael was delighted with him. Many years later, Michael remembered the very first time John came over to the house on 20 Forthlin Road. "By a million-to-one chance I'm in the front parlor and I looked up, and saw this Teddy

Boy. Wow, he looked so good . . . and, hold on, he's coming up down our path—past me dad's lavender bush. He looks good!"

Raising two teenagers without Mary to rely on was hard, and Jim had to come up with parenting strategies of his own. First and foremost, he decided, father and sons should live by the twin principles of tolerance and moderation. He understood Paul well enough to know that putting his foot down would just make his son rebel. Jim suspected, for instance, that Paul had flunked his Latin exams the previous spring because Jim had kept insisting they were important. John Lennon, he feared, was just the match to spark a more serious rebellion.

So though he made his disapproval known, Jim allowed the Quarry Men to practice at their house. The dining room off the kitchen, with the table pushed up against the wall, offered a nice-sized space for the band, especially since Colin and his drum kit weren't usually invited because Jim worried the thumping would annoy the neighbors.

Paul's debut with the Quarry Men took place on October 18, 1957, at the New Clubmoor Hall in the Norris Green area of Liverpool, where they performed for members of the Conservative Club. Nigel had fixed it up with a local band promoter, Charlie McBain, and was told that if the evening's performance went well, there might be other bookings.

Hooking up with a local promoter was a big deal, and John decided that the guys needed to polish their look. There was talk of white jackets over their black jeans. When it came time to buy the jackets, though, only two were purchased—for John and Paul. To add insult to injury, everyone was expected to chip in on the cost, leaving a grumbling Nigel to collect shillings every week. Photos taken at the time show John and Paul in their white jackets, playing their guitars and singing into the mike, with the others, jacketless, in the background.

The Quarry Men at one of the earliest performances with Paul in the band.

Besides practicing with his bandmates, Paul had been spending his free time brushing up on the chords he was learning and practicing new songs. "For my first gig," he said, looking back, "I was given a guitar solo on 'Guitar Boogie.' I could play it easily in rehearsal, so they elected that I should do it as my solo. Things were going fine, but when the moment came in the performance I got sticky fingers, I thought, 'What am I doing here?' I was just too frightened; it was too big a moment with everyone looking at the guitar player. I couldn't do it."

Paul experienced an emotion he wasn't very familiar with—humiliation. His bandmates were surprised at how he fumbled the chords. "At first, we were embarrassed," says Colin Hanton. "Just really uncomfortable with what had happened. John insisted on a certain degree of professionalism." Colin expected a swift reaction from John, and John did shoot Paul a sharp look, but he let the flub pass without comment, at least in front of the others.

Perhaps what the rest of the band didn't know was how close John and Paul were becoming. From their meeting at the summer fête, John had been impressed by Paul's guitar-playing abilities, which far exceeded his own. As soon as Paul agreed to join the Quarry Men, John began spending time alone with him, learning how to play properly.

In later years, John wouldn't say Paul was more talented, only that his musical education was better, but he did admit that his guitar playing would have hit a dead end without Paul.

"I could only play the mouth organ and two chords on a guitar when we met. I tuned the guitar like a banjo, so my guitar only had five strings on it. Paul taught me how to play properly, but I had to learn the chords left-handed because Paul is left-handed. So I learnt them upside down and I'd go home and reverse them."

Paul remembers sitting in John's small bedroom at the top of the house—a poster of French movie star Brigitte Bardot taped on the wall—facing John as they plucked chords. They would do the same at his house. They learned as much as they could from their practice sessions, but they didn't stop there. They discovered new recording artists, ran down obscure rock records, and once took a bus into a dangerous part of Liverpool just because they heard someone there knew how to play the difficult B7 chord and might be willing to show them how it was done.

John's small bedroom featured a large poster of actress Brigitte Bardot.

It was at this time that Paul and John also began trying to write their own songs, a process that would help cement their relationship.

Paul, seeing that John was as passionate about music as he was and knowing he appreciated anyone who showed real talent, decided it was time to introduce John to George Harrison, the best guitar player Paul knew. He didn't mention it to John, but Paul could see George joining the Quarry Men. There was just one problem. George was only fourteen.

George lived on the Speke estate, and the two had known each other casually there. After Paul moved, the boys took the same bus to school once George followed Paul to the Inny in 1954. As soon as they started talking, it was clear they were both wild about music in general and guitars in particular.

Before George ever owned one, he would draw pictures of guitars in a notebook when he should have been listening in class. Like Paul, John, and so many others, rock and roll blew him away. And just like Paul and John, he remembered the first time he heard Elvis Presley sing. "I was riding along on my bicycle and heard 'Heartbreak Hotel' coming out of somebody's house. It was one of them things I'll never forget: what a sound, what a record! It changed the course of my life."

George, the youngest of four children, lived with his bus-driver dad, Harry, and his mother, Louise, who worked at a greengrocer. Louise, in particular, was supportive of whatever he wanted to do, so when George went to his mom and asked if he could buy an Egmond guitar a friend was selling cheap, she agreed. Almost as soon as he got it, he broke off a piece, and in disgust, he tossed it in the cupboard.

He couldn't get guitars out of his mind, however, especially with all the great rock music that just kept coming. Finally, he asked his older brother to fix the guitar, and once he did, George started playing and barely put the instrument down. He took a couple of lessons, but then he was on his own. Louise said he would practice until his fingers started to bleed.

Like Paul, who'd first practiced with his pal Ian, George had a friend named Arthur Kelley with whom he'd get together and try to figure out chords, while listening to rock music in the background. It didn't take him long to realize he needed a better guitar, and once again he prevailed on Louise, this time to finance a Hofner President. It cost more than the family could really afford, but Louise scraped together the money, and George proved her confidence in his ability wasn't misplaced. "I would sit around for hours, playing and trying to figure things out . . . I used to sit up late at night. I didn't look on it as practicing, more learning . . . I'd polish the guitar and clean it and make it really impeccable."

The first time George heard the Quarry Men play was at another performance Charlie McBain had arranged at Wilson Hall in a tough part of town. Getting to and from gigs wasn't easy, since the group had to rely on buses to get them back and forth between the Penny Lane roundabout and wherever they were headed in Liverpool or the surrounding areas. They all had to take their instruments on board—even Colin and his mini drum kit—and store them in the luggage area behind the bus driver. When coming home from the more dangerous areas, the boys always made sure they knew exactly what time the last bus was heading back home.

There are different versions of George's first meeting with John, but it seems George just said hello to him at the Wilson Hall appearance. Then, in the early days of 1958, John, pushed by Paul, actually listened to George play. Some remember it happening on the upper deck of a bus; others think it was at a rehearsal that George came to. Colin Hanton has a memory of it being at a skiffle club called the Morgue. But everyone remembers that the song George played was "Raunchy," a guitar solo that was even more complicated than "Twenty Flight Rock," the song that Paul had played to impress the Quarry Men at the fête.

John had to admit that George was good—very good—but he wasn't thrilled about adding him to the group. "I didn't dig him on first sight. George looked even younger than Paul and Paul looked about ten with his baby face. It was too much. George was just too young." He added, "I didn't dig him till I got to know him." That took a while. The college student had no time for a kid just about to turn fifteen, but George was patient. He would turn up at gigs and come to rehearsals, happily filling in if someone didn't show up.

Not surprisingly, Mimi didn't approve of George. Small and thin with a lot of gelled hair and a wolfish grin, he dressed as a Ted, pushing the boundaries of his school uniform by adding pointy shoes called winkle pickers and wearing bright shirts under his uniform. Mimi may have had to look hard to find fault with Paul, but George was an easy target, especially with his thick scouse accent. "You always seem to like the lower-class types, don't you, John?" she'd say with disgust.

Jim, on the other hand, liked George, who was a welcome visitor at the McCartney house. They had developed a warm relationship based on George's appreciation for music from earlier eras and his readiness to happily devour whatever Jim cooked—he was especially fond of his custard.

John may have been reluctant to ask George to join the Quarry Men, but knowing the band needed a guitar soloist now that Paul was no longer comfortable after the "Guitar Boogie" fiasco, he agreed in early 1958 that George should come aboard. As much as John wanted George's expertise for the band, he was also eager to take in everything he could from George's knowledge about chords in particular and guitar playing in general. John wasn't one to show vulnerability much, but he did admit years later that he didn't know what he didn't know until he watched his new bandmates. "All I ever wanted to do was vamp [repeat familiar chords], then George and Paul came along and taught me other things."

As for Paul, who knew how to subtly manipulate a situation when he wanted to—and he often wanted to—he was thrilled to have maneuvered George into the band, both for his talent and his friendship. "He had a great sense of himself. He wasn't cowed by anything." Paul also didn't mind that now there was a Quarry Man younger than he was.

For his part, George seemed immune to the idea he was somehow lesser than his bandmates. "I was asked by John to join the group, I didn't twist his arm." Yes, his relationship with John was complicated by their age difference, but he had no problem standing up to John or trading barbs with him. "He was very sarcastic, always trying to bring you down, but I either took no notice or gave him the same back and it worked."

George also didn't mind voicing his opinion once he was on the scene. He made it clear that he didn't think there was any more need for Eric Griffiths and his middling guitar playing. With now four guitar players, John and Paul were coming to the same conclusion. Still, it was awkward to just kick out one of the original Quarry Men. So Paul and John came up with an elaborate scheme. First, they started "forgetting" to invite Eric to rehearsals. Then, they told him that to stay in the group he needed to show his commitment by buying an expensive electric guitar and amp.

Eric had neither the money nor even the desire to do that. In a particularly cowardly move, Paul and John tossed the job of telling Eric he was out to Nigel, insisting that since he was the band manager (who took the same cut of money they did) it was his job to fire Eric. Nigel remembered the actual meeting as being as sad and awkward as he feared.

Since Colin had come to the band through Eric, the firing left a bad taste with him, and the drummer soon began skipping rehearsals. As for Len, whose tea-chest bass screamed skiffle, not rock, he would have been pushed out as well if he hadn't developed a case of tubercular meningitis requiring months to recuperate.

There was one addition to the group, which was still using the name Quarry Men, although John was the only one left with an affiliation to the school. John "Duff" Lowe was added as a piano player, but he could only play clubs and halls that had a piano available. Duff's father was strict when it came to curfew, and sometimes he had to duck out early, leaving an empty piano bench before the set was over.

In the summer of 1958, the group decided to make a record. George, who often hung out with other musicians, had learned about a local recording studio. Kensington Records was run by a man named Percy Phillips out of his home in a Victorian townhouse. It wasn't much of a studio, just a microphone hanging from the ceiling and rugs and blankets tacked on the walls to muffle outside traffic noises. Nevertheless, the idea of recording was thrilling, and the boys thought it was a neat piece of symmetry that the owner of Kensington was named Phillips since Sam Phillips was the head of Sun Records, Elvis's recording studio in Memphis.

The official date of the recording is July 15, 1958, but some remember it being earlier in the summer. What is certain is that John, Paul, George, Colin, and Duff all came up with their share of the seventeen shillings that the recording cost. For that, they would get one 78-rpm record, with labels on the front and back, tucked in its own brown paper sleeve.

The "A" side of the record was the Quarry Men's cover of Buddy Holly's "That'll Be the Day." The music of Buddy Holly and the Crickets arrived in England in the autumn of 1957, and it made a huge impression on John, Paul, and George. Holly had it all—a distinct sound, the ability to sing and play the guitar at the same time (not just strum like Elvis), and he wrote his own songs. The British public took to the group, not just for the music, but because the name *Crickets* conjured up the popular English sport cricket. There was one more reason John Lennon, in particular, loved Buddy Holly. Holly proudly wore his black horn-rimmed glasses on and off the stage. For John, who'd bump into walls before putting on his specs, Holly's attitude was a revelation, and it liberated John to wear his similarly styled glasses—not often, but once in a while.

The "B" side of the recording was a song called "In Spite of All the Danger," which was written by Paul and featured a long guitar solo performed by George. John sang the lead on both songs, and years later he noted that his ego was so big that he wouldn't even let Paul sing the lead on his own song. Those who've heard the record give John props for a credible rock rendition, with Paul providing solid harmony. Years later, Paul recalled what the session was like. "I remember we all went down on the bus with our instruments, amps, and guitars, and the drummer went separately. We waited in a little waiting room outside while somebody else made their demo and then it was our turn. We just went into the room, hardly saw the feller because he was next door in a little control booth . . . We ran through it very quickly . . . and it was all over."

Since they only had enough money for one precious record, they decided that first John, then Paul, George, Colin, and Duff would get it for a week each. After a go-around, the record ended up with Duff, who still only played sporadically with the band. At some point, he packed it away.

As John, Paul, and George's fame grew in the coming years, their first recording was being called the most valuable record ever made, with estimates of its worth rising to hundreds of thousands of British pounds. Duff learned that Paul, who liked to collect memorabilia from his early years as a musician, wanted to buy it, though probably not for that amount. Rather than sell it for the highest possible bid, Duff chose to sell it to Paul for a more reasonable sum, about $25,000. Still, not a bad return on the investment of a few shillings.

It might seem odd that the excitement of making a recording faded so quickly. No one knows for sure, but there may have been a tragic reason the boys forgot about the record. On a hot July evening, John's mother, Julia, was hit by a car while crossing Menlove Avenue after a visit with Mimi. She died upon impact, sprawled on the pavement as if asleep, her wavy hair blowing in the breeze.

Let It Be

"I WAS STAYING with Julia and Twitchy this weekend. We were sitting waiting for her to come home, Twitchy and me, wondering why she was late. The copper came to the door, to tell us about the accident. It was just like it's supposed to be, the way it is in the films. Asking if I were her son, and all that. Then he told us, we both went white. It was the worst thing that ever happened to me."

Paul may not have known his mother was going to die, but her surgery and hospitalization alerted him to serious issues with Mary's health. For John, news of Julia's death was a shock to the soul.

"We got a taxi over to Sefton General where she was lying dead . . . I talked hysterically to the taxi driver all the way, just ranted on and on . . . I refused to go in and see her."

In a cruel twist of fate, Nigel Walley was the last person to see Julia alive. He had stopped by Mimi's to see John. "Mimi said John was out, then

Julia said, 'Oh, Nigel, you've arrived in time to escort me to the bus stop.'" Nigel was happy to take a stroll with the vivacious Julia. They said their goodbyes, and he turned off at Vale Road toward home, and she headed across Menlove Avenue to the bus stop. "At that moment I heard a car skidding and a thump, and I turned to see her body fling through the air. I rushed over."

Mimi and her boarder, Michael Fishwick, hearing the screech of wheels, rushed outside. "There was Julia," he remembered, "looking quite peaceful, bloodied only at the back of her head." Passersby stopped, someone called an ambulance, but it was clear Julia's accident was fatal.

Julia's death was not only a nightmare for John; it turned life upside down for his half sisters, Julia, eleven, and Jackie, eight. One of the first things out of Bobby Dykins's mouth when he heard Julia had died was to ask who was going to take care of the girls now. Even in his grief, John was shocked by the comment. The answer to that question turned out to be not their father. The girls were sent to Scotland to be with family, without being told Julia was dead, only that she was in the hospital. After a month, they came home to the truth; they also found out that their father was giving custody of them to Julia and Mimi's sister Harriet and her husband. They never lived with Bobby again.

What John did not know was the reason for Julia's visit to Mimi's that night; if he had, it would have torn him up even further. Bobby Dykins had been ticketed several weeks earlier for drunk driving and had lost his license. Unable to drive, he wasn't able to keep the late hours his restaurant job in the city center demanded. With no money coming in, Bobby quickly became exasperated with John's hearty appetite and his habit of asking his mother for spending money. Bobby told Julia things had to change and ordered her to make sure her son spent less time at their house. It must have pained Julia, but she went to Mimi's that July evening to tell her sister about Bobby's demand and discuss how to break the news to John.

The funeral took place on July 21, 1958, at Allerton Cemetery. Afterward, the mourners went back to Aunt Harriet's house for tea and sandwiches. There is only one report of how John dealt with that day, and it came from his cousin Leila. "John and I just sat there on the couch. I never said a word . . . I can't even recall telling him I was sorry. There was nothing you could say. We were both numb with anguish."

Julia's accident had been caused by an off-duty policeman, who only had a learner's permit and should not have been in the car alone. In later years, John would say the man was drunk, but that wasn't true. The inquest into the death ruled it was the driver's inexperience, rather than alcohol, that was responsible for his inability to control the car as Julia stepped through the hedge that separated the four lanes of Menlove Avenue traffic and crossed into the street.

Nigel and Mimi struggled with their guilt. Both went over and over the night's events, knowing that if one of them had only kept Julia talking for a few more minutes, she wouldn't have been crossing the street at just the wrong moment. And while John's dependence on Mimi spared her from his blame, he did take his anger out on Nigel, ripping a hole in their lifelong friendship.

Ironically, it had only been a few weeks earlier, during a practice session at the Harrison house, when George's mother, Louise, heard John mutter, for no apparent reason, that he didn't know how Paul acted so normally when his mother was dead. "If anything like that happened to me, I'd go off my head." Now it was his turn to deal with a parent's death.

John was shaken to his core, but he threw on a hard shell. Pete Shotton found out the news from Nigel, and when he awkwardly offered his condolences—"Sorry about your mum"—John reacted quietly: "I know." And nothing more was said. With others, John wouldn't discuss it at all. That didn't mean people didn't see the change in John that happened after Julia's death.

The cruel streak that had always been a part of John's personality now became more pronounced. Admitting later that he had had a huge chip on his shoulder, John was bitter and biting, taking his pain out on those in whom he saw weakness. One of the final incidents that pushed Colin to leave the band was when John made fun of a deaf couple using sign language on a bus. Colin, who had deaf friends, was disgusted. John was always more verbally abusive when he drank, and that was a problem, because now he was drinking a lot. His girlfriend at the time, Thelma Pickles, was a frequent victim of his anger, with the abuse once turning physical. She broke up with John, yelling, "Don't blame me just because your mother's dead!"

The one release valve for John was his music. For a short time, he had thought maybe he would find his way in art school when one of the school's most revered teachers, Arthur Ballard, took an interest in him. Ballard had come across one of John's notebooks filled with caricatures and wordplay, and he was gobsmacked by its originality. "I was absolutely amazed! It showed so much talent." Ballard took it upon himself to take the notebook to the school administrators to argue that John should be moved into illustration courses. But the higher-ups, who had already pigeonholed Lennon as disruptive and unworthy of special attention, turned down Ballard's request.

If he was disappointed that his chance of a career in art was unlikely at best, John pretended he wasn't. There was still rock and roll. Bookings, though, were not as plentiful as they were before. With Colin gone and Duff drifting away, the band was now, basically, three guitar players. For a brief time, Michael McCartney sat in on rehearsals, playing drums, but the arm he'd broken at scout camp had not healed properly and hampered his playing. More professional drummers were in demand around Liverpool and expected payment, something the band could not guarantee.

Even so, Paul, ever the entrepreneur, tried to pitch three guitarists as a plus not a minus. When pursuing gigs, he would tell those hiring that the rhythm was in the guitars, and so drums weren't needed. In a surviving letter, he writes to a journalist in an effort to get some publicity, "This lineup may at first seem dull, but it must be appreciated that as the boys have above-average instrumental ability, they achieve surprisingly varied effects." You had to admire his bravado, but nobody was buying it.

The few gigs they had in late 1958 demanded a new name for the band, and they came up with several. For a moment, they were the Rainbows and wore different-colored shirts. They tried out Japage 3, using letters from their first names with an added *a*. It turned out to be a name no one could pronounce and had the unfortunate aspect of the first three letters spelling out *Jap*, a derogatory nickname for Japanese people that was common during World War II. It was under the name Johnny and the Moondogs, though, that the trio had their shot at stardom.

Once again, it was London's Carroll Levis who came calling in 1958, this time looking to make stars out of local talent for his show called *TV Star Search*. It had been almost eighteen months since John and the Quarry Men had auditioned for Levis, before Paul's and George's time with the band. The show really had boosted some of its winners into national

Paul and John (far right) playing at the Casbah Club in 1958. The fans' enthusiastic reaction to their music gave them their first real taste of fame.

prominence, so the lads were thrilled when they got through a preliminary round and were asked to perform on November 8, in Manchester, after passing the first audition.

Johnny and the Moondogs brought George's friend Arthur Kelley along that evening for moral support, and he remembered the group putting on a stellar performance, singing Buddy Holly's song "Think It Over." Since John's "guaranteed not to split" guitar had recently done just that—in its defense, it had taken quite a beating, being hauled around

Liverpool on buses—only Paul and George played while John sang.

They won enough applause to come back for a playoff at the show's end, but when their name was called, they weren't present. The last train for Liverpool left the Manchester Central station at 10:25, and they had no money to eat or stay over, or even buy an expensive morning train ticket. Johnny and the Moondogs, plus Arthur, angrily ran to get their train, never knowing if stardom had been snatched from their grasp.

10

I'm Down

PAUL TRIED TO be a life preserver for John, but immediately after Julia's death, there was little he could do to get through to his friend. "Julia was the light of John's life; he idolized her," he said. These feelings were similar to those Paul had for his mother, Mary. If anyone understood John's pain, it was Paul, so he mostly waited, just letting John know he would be there when he was ready.

With music on hold for the moment, Paul had time to think about the future. A friend once said about John that either he'd be amazingly successful or he'd be a tramp. No one would have ever thought that about Paul. Yes, he was mesmerized by rock, and yes, he'd probably be a musician if he could, but he didn't think it was his only option. Paul had been a solid student when he'd first entered the Liverpool Institute with good

Paul with his father, Jim, and brother, Michael, in the garden behind their house in 1960.

grades and the coronation essay win under his belt, but after years of falling marks and many days of skipping school, his star had dimmed. When he took his O-level exams, he passed in English and art. His teachers no longer thought he'd be going to a top university like Oxford or Cambridge, but they still thought he could find a place at a local teachers college. Being a teacher was a job his father encouraged.

In fact, Paul had a number of options open to him. Although his artistic talent had never really been nurtured, he was an excellent artist, and a more disciplined one than John. He was a fine writer and an avid reader of newspapers, so he might have gone into journalism. His interests ranged further than his bandmates' as well. He would go to the Liverpool Playhouse and the Royal Court theaters by himself, and he would buy (or sometimes steal) books from local bookshops. The books' authors included John Steinbeck, Dylan Thomas, and Samuel Beckett. "I was quite a lone wolf . . . I'd take a bus to the Pier Head [at the Liverpool docks], go on the ferry by myself. I'd take a book of poetry, or a play, or something to read . . . [I'd] think of myself as a bit of a poet, observing people, sit on a bench and write a little bit of what I saw. I was very conscious of gathering material. I didn't know then what it would be for . . . my mind was full of it; it was an intoxication."

John's mood in the early months of 1959 matched the gray cold of a Liverpool winter.

Paul tried to get him to practice, but the sessions were few and far between; actual gigs were even scarcer. George became so disenchanted with the band's prospects, he tried hooking up with other musicians, which he called "freelancing." He did get gigs here and there, but it wasn't anything like playing with his friends.

Not having many chances to play onstage was only one of George's problems. In the spring of 1959, he failed all of his prep O-levels, except for art. He had already decided that school wasn't for him, but this was proof. Unbeknownst to his parents, he skipped his classes for the rest of the term, and in the summer, he dropped out of the Liverpool Institute. George's disappointed father, Harry, tried to get him fixed up as an apprentice electrician, but he failed that test, too. George wound up working for a local department store putting together window displays.

Despite John's continued moodiness, rudeness, and drinking—"I was in a sort of blind rage for about two years"—his friends tried to help. There was a hip little coffee bar near school called the Jacaranda, run by Allan and Beryl Williams. They were only a decade or so older than the art college kids but took an almost-parental interest in them. John and his art-school pal Stuart Sutcliffe would often park themselves in the back of the bar and talk for hours, with John venting about his loss and feelings of abandonment. He could not deal with the fact, as he put it, he had lost his mother twice. When Buddy Holly was killed in airplane crash on February 3, 1959, John was shocked but not surprised. People you love die.

Stu also helped by letting John crash at his apartment now and again. As a college student, John felt he had outgrown his small bedroom at Mimi's, even though he would sneak girls up there when she left Mendips for her weekly bridge game. He wasn't happy either about relying on her for his expenses—but not so unhappy that he wanted to get a job. As for Mimi, she was hassling him less about music. Perhaps it was because she felt so bad about the effect Julia's death had on him, or maybe she thought he was doing better in art school than he really was, but she decided to act as if guitar playing were just a phase.

There must have been times during the first half of 1959 that thought crossed the boys' minds as well. Gigs were still few and far between, though Allan Williams did let them play now and again on the Jacaranda's ridiculously small stage. There was even less money coming in than there were jobs. The only bright spot musically was that John and Paul started writing together again.

Finally, during the summer, light appeared in John's dark, emotional night. At an end-of-the-term get-together at the art college in July, John danced with Cynthia Powell. After all the months of ignoring her or making cutting remarks, or just being friendly, John suddenly saw her in a whole new light. For her part, Cynthia had realized a few months earlier that she had a crush on John, and though his brusque and cutting manner could be frightening, she found him exciting as well. From that night on, John and Cynthia were a couple.

She didn't know, at first, that his mother had recently died, and when she found out, she was even more determined to be a safe place for John to land. Cynthia understood what it meant to lose a parent because her own father had died a few years earlier. John's jealousy and possessiveness was a problem, however. "He was full of contradictions and confusion. He wanted proof, daily, that he mattered most to me . . . Yet despite John's aggression and jealousy, I felt protective towards him. To me he was a lost soul and I wanted to give him understanding, acceptance, and the security of being loved to ease his pain and bitterness."

To please him even more, Cynthia dyed her light brown hair blond and put it up in a beehive hairdo, à la Brigitte Bardot, and she changed her conservative clothes to short skirts and tight sweaters.

John's tender side, usually kept hidden, was revealed to Cynthia. He wrote her poetry and love notes, all illustrated with his clever cartoons. But he would also rage, once hitting her after she had danced with someone else. That was too much for Cynthia, and she broke up with him.

Cynthia and John in 1964. A rare photo of him wearing his horn-rimmed glasses.

After a few weeks, he called, promising never to do that again and asking for another chance. He kept his word, but his anger remained close to the surface, and Cynthia nervously tried to make sure that nothing upset him.

All of this support took a toll on Cynthia. Once an excellent student, her grades began to fall. Her widowed mother was not pleased, and yet again, like almost every parent before her, Mrs. Powell was dismayed by the presence of John Lennon in her child's life. More surprising was Mimi's reaction to Cynthia. A well-spoken, middle-class girl would seem to be just what Mimi would have had in mind for John, but the truth was plain by now—Mimi viewed anyone who got close to John as a rival for his affection. To make matters worse, when Mimi and Cynthia's mother met for tea, tempers flared, with each arguing that her child was too good for the other. Having the two women closest to them dislike each other made it hard for John and Cynthia, but they didn't let the animosity stand in their way. They were besotted with one another.

After a musical drought so long there was almost no band to break up, a new opportunity came along in the summer of 1959. Teen clubs had been springing up all over—places where, for a few shillings' membership, young people could enjoy rock music and nonalcoholic drinks. Mona Best, the wife of a local boxing entrepreneur, decided to open one in the basement of her fifteen-room Victorian mansion where her son, Pete, and his friends could go.

The club, to be christened the Casbah Coffee Club, needed a house band, and George asked Mona Best if he, John, and Paul could play there. Mona agreed to take them on if they would help finish painting the club, to which they all happily agreed. Cynthia helped, too, painting a silhouette of John on one of the walls. John, who had spent some of the summer working in a factory to earn enough money to buy a guitar, purchased a Hofner 40 for the new gig. He bought it on the installment plan, and since he was only a student, he needed an adult cosigner. After arguing about his guitar playing for years, John had finally worn Mimi down. She was his cosigner.

Since none of their other band names had panned out, John, George, and Paul went back to being the Quarry Men for their Casbah debut. They played at the club's opening on August 29, 1959, and as Cynthia remembered, "about three hundred people came along that night, and the boys played rock and roll for a couple of hours. The place heaved, and with kids jibing and swinging, and the temperature soared until it was hard to breathe." The Casbah was everything young people could want in a club: a noisy, smoky, packed place that reverberated with the sound of rock.

Paul once said the reason to join a band was to get a girl, and he found one at the Casbah. Sixteen-year-old Dot Rhone first had her eye on John, but when she found out about Cynthia, her attention shifted to Paul. Waif-like yet determined, Dot caught Paul's eye when she pretended to faint in front of him in the packed club. In short order, they were a couple, with Paul the concerned, protective boyfriend. But like John, he could be intimidating when he wanted, making Dot feel, as Cynthia did with John, that it was her job to keep the relationship running smoothly. Although both couples considered themselves going steady, John and Paul didn't try very hard to distance themselves from the many girls who wanted to get close to a boy in a band. But if it seemed like Dot or Cynthia was paying attention to other guys, they went ballistic. Cynthia said she was afraid she was doing something wrong about 75 percent of the time. Yet in a male-dominated place like Liverpool in the 1950s, having to bend to a boyfriend's will did not seem particularly odd.

The Quarry Men's job as a house band lasted for a couple of months. It was a great opportunity to play in front of big crowds, hone their act, and establish a fan base. Mona was thrilled as the club's memberships went up and up. Then, in the late fall, there was a silly dispute over money. Mona insisted on paying a musician who was too sick to play his set. The Quarry Men thought that was unprofessional—no play, no pay—but Mona Best was not the sort of woman to back down, so the boys left in a huff. The Casbah survived; for the Quarry Men, it meant the end of a good thing, though they did occasionally play there again in the years that followed. There would be one more link to the club. Mona's good-looking son, Pete, who had been watching the Quarry Men with keen interest, decided to take up the drums. Whether it was because he noticed the band could use a drummer, it's hard to say. But a year later, he did join them under yet another new name, the Beatles.

A surprising addition to the group came at the very end of 1959: Stu Sutcliffe. Slight, intense Stu and the wilder John had developed a deep friendship, one that seemed odd to those who knew them. Stu was as focused and dedicated to art school as John was disorganized and uncaring. But each found something important in their differences. John was in awe of Stu's artistic talent and his work ethic, while introspective Stu fed off of John's energy and confidence. John, who always wanted to appear as if he were in control, for once let Stu take the lead when it came to art. In the last months of 1959, he tried to learn as much as he could about serious painting from his friend, and Stu was a willing teacher.

Everyone in the school, students and teachers, knew that Stu was destined for big things in the art world. Yet there was still surprise when he won an important art contest and sold the prize painting for $150, a huge amount for an art student. (Paul won an art prize around the same time, but the only person who seemed very interested in that was Jim McCartney, who came to the Liverpool Institute to see his son accept the award.)

Surprise turned to shock when word got around the school that somehow John had talked Stu into using the prize money to buy a Hofner bass guitar, an instrument Stu could barely play. Several of the teachers were particularly upset, wondering why such a talented artist would want to fool around with music when he could be devoting his time (and prize money) to his craft. But Stu was excited to be joining a band. Like so many of John's friends before him, Stu was delighted to be in John's inner circle, experiencing the heightened reality that seemed to wrap itself around John.

Finally, John's mood seemed to be lightening. For their first Christmas together, John made a charming card for Cynthia with cartoons of them, dotted by hearts and kisses. It delighted her both for the romantic senti-

Stu, John, Paul, and George onstage in Liverpool, 1960. They did not have a regular drummer, so Johnny Hutch sat in.

ment and as a visible symbol of their relationship. As Cynthia saw it, there were only two other people as close to John as she was—Stu Sutcliffe and Paul McCartney.

Yet as important as the friendship between John and Stu was, and as exciting as the relationship of John and Cynthia was, ultimately these did not compare to the bond between John Lennon and Paul McCartney. This was a relationship that would last longer and be more intense than those John had with either Cynthia or Stu. Music was the centerpiece in John's life, and its importance would surpass a brotherly bond or even romantic love.

The Long and Winding Road

THE 1950S WERE drawing to a close. A shiny new decade was about to begin. There wasn't a soul who thought that it would be defined, in part, by a Liverpool band. How did that happen?

The boys made great music, but so did plenty of bands. They worked hard to improve themselves; so did most musicians. And, of course, there was an element of luck to their success, just as there is for any actor, singer, writer, or musician who takes their star power into the stratosphere. But for John Lennon and Paul McCartney, it was their magnetic connection, creative and competitive in equal parts, that elevated their music. This chemistry was most apparent in their role as songwriters.

After John's struggle with the loss of Julia, Paul and John resumed their songwriting. As the coming years would show, they had a unique ability, given to very few, to write music that resonates across decades and impacts people throughout their lives. Had someone told them this at the time, they would probably have laughed and said, "Are you taking the mickey, then?"—using a British phrase that means putting someone on or making fun of them.

Songwriting—at least the kind of songwriting that lasts—wasn't something they would have associated with folks from Liverpool. Because both boys, especially Paul, had grown up listening to adult popular music, they were aware of legendary songwriters like George Gershwin, Rodgers and Hammerstein, and Cole Porter, but that kind of talent and fame seemed very far away. Rock singers, they quickly learned, rarely wrote their own songs. Certainly, Elvis Presley did not.

And yet, even before they met, Paul and John were coming up with songs. Paul's "I've Lost My Little Girl" and "Calypso Rock," a tune John wrote, were both penned within months of first picking up a guitar. So perhaps it's not so surprising that back in 1957, when Paul and John first started getting together to learn chords, practice songs, and listen to records, their sessions quickly included writing songs. Paul recalled how it all began: "One day the conversation went, 'You know, I've written one or two songs.' And he said, 'Yeah, so have I' . . . And then the logical extension was, 'Well, maybe we could write one together.' So that's how we started." Creating music became the most important element in their unique bond. There were so many facets to their process: inspiration, collaboration, dedication, and always plenty of laughs.

Even though, in the early days, Mimi and Jim McCartney were equally unenthused about the boys' burgeoning friendship, there was one difference in the beginning: Mimi was at home to disapprove; Jim had to go to work each day, leaving the McCartney house empty. Sometimes the boys would go to Mendips, sitting on the bed next to each other in John's small bedroom, but despite the fun of learning together, the space really wasn't made for two teenagers and bulky guitars. "Physically, it was always a bad idea for us to sit side by side on the bed," Paul recalled. "The necks of our guitars were always banging."

What they did like, when Mimi was out, was to take their guitars into the glass-enclosed vestibule and sing and play. The acoustics, thanks to the glass and high ceiling, made them sound great. Knocking out Elvis's version of "Blue Moon" was one of John's favorite memories of singing there. Mostly, though, it was easier to head over to Paul's house. Of course, the boys were supposed to be at school, but John had freedom at art school, and Paul wasn't opposed to skipping out of class at the Inny—"sagging off," as he called it. Together, they would clamber onto the number 86 bus that took them out of the city and left them off near Forthlin Road, where they had the house to themselves until Jim came home from work about six o'clock.

Before they'd begin playing, they'd raid the icebox and check to see if Jim had left any cigarette butts lying around. If not, they'd grab a couple of his pipes, and if they couldn't find any tobacco, they'd smoke pipes filled with tea leaves, which made them feel cool, but tasted awful. Paul remembered, "We had to waft all the tea-tobacco smell away . . . before my dad came home and caught us." If they couldn't immediately settle down, John would use the McCartney telephone for prank calls. He particularly liked using his former headmaster's name, Pobjoy, when making the calls, just because he thought it was so silly.

The seating arrangement in the small McCartney living room made it necessary for the boys to sit on chairs opposite each other, practically "nose to nose" as John put it. "Because I was left-handed, when I looked at John, I would see almost a mirror image of myself," Paul remembered. They'd watch each other to see how they were playing the new chords they were learning. "It was quite a useful visual aid."

It hadn't taken John and Paul long to discover how perfectly their voices meshed, with Paul's lighter voice taking the higher harmonies, and John's nasal and harder-edged sound more suitable for the lower tones. But sounding good together was easy. Writing songs was harder.

They soon decided the only way to do it was to start. Paul said, "We'd sit down and say, OK, what we are going to do? And we just start off strumming and one or the other of us would kick off some kind of idea and then we'd just develop and bounce off each other."

Their first songs were their own takes on the rock music they were listening to. Buddy Holly was a particular inspiration because he was one singer who did write his own songs. He used only a few simple chords, which made it easier for John and Paul to try and emulate him. As they tried out different ideas, it quickly became clear they would have to figure out a way to capture them on paper.

Paul found a blue school exercise book and on the first page wrote, "A Lennon-McCartney Original." As they wrote more during the fall of 1957, each page became "Another Lennon-McCartney Original." They had decided almost immediately that's how their songwriting credit would read. The letter *L* comes before *M* in the alphabet, so that was one reason for the order, but mostly it was because John was always first among equals.

They scribbled down ideas and words, which they would then try to set to tunes. Back and forth they'd bounce these elements between each other, until something emerged that might be called a song. Since neither of them could read music and tape cassettes had not yet been invented, there was no real way to capture their musical efforts. They tried to indicate the melody by writing down the chords they'd played. But both of them decided that, if they couldn't remember a song the next day, they'd chuck it, on the theory that if they couldn't remember it, there was no reason anyone else would.

They also agreed that even if they wrote songs individually, the music would be called Lennon-McCartney compositions. It was odd that two teens just starting to write, who had no immediate role models, would even think about who'd receive credit for their music, but this decision would have wide-ranging implications in the future when they became successful. Part of their reasoning was that even when writing alone, they always came to each other for suggestions, critiques, and encouragement, so almost every tune was touched by both of them.

John and Paul loved the writing process. "It was great," Paul recalled, "because instead of looking into my own mind for a song, I could see John playing." Once again, Paul used the image of a mirror to capture the experience: "[It was] as if he was holding a mirror to what I was doing." John remembered the excitement of finding the right hook that would make the song zing. "And Paul hits this chord, and I turn to him and say, 'That's it! Do that again.'"

One of the most surprising things about their collaborations was how quickly they wrote. Since they only had a couple of hours alone at a time, they made sure to come up with something at each session. This practice of making the use of their time continued for years, long after they had plenty of time and space to write. Those around them were always amazed how John and Paul could pick up their guitars, whether on a tour bus, in a hotel room, or just lounging about, and plow through until they had come up with a tune.

Paul claimed in a letter he had written to get some publicity that he and John had written almost one hundred songs. By the beginning of 1959, the actual number was closer to fifteen. For teenagers who couldn't properly write music, this was still an excellent output, and some good, solid songs came out of that early collaboration. Among them were "I Call Your Name," a bluesy tune that John started writing in his bedroom; "The One after 909," one of their earliest efforts, about a young man who misses getting together with his girl because he's not sure which train she's on; "I'll Follow the Sun," a song Paul wrote looking out his living room window after a rainstorm; and "Love Me Do," a joint effort that became one of the Beatles' earliest hits.

The more comfortable they became writing together, the more things they found to write. For a brief time, they decided to write a play about a Jesus-like figure named Pilchard who everyone keeps waiting for but never appears. They were excited by the idea but quit a few pages in. "We couldn't quite figure out how playwrights did it," Paul recalled later. "Did they work it all out and work through the chapters, or did they just write a stream of consciousness like we were doing?"

Paul also collaborated with John on comic writings done in *The Daily Howl* fashion. Both of them were still in love with wordplay and happily riffed off each other as they concocted elaborate stories and poems that had their seeds in Lewis Carroll's poetry. One was the tale of a safari hunter: "Jumble Jim, who shall remain nameless, was slowly but slowly asking his way through the underpants." These were created in John's bedroom, which now boasted a typewriter. Paul was beyond impressed. He had never seen a typewriter outside a business office.

It was a good thing that Paul and John had their writing experiences to use as a glue to keep them together. Without them, their musical careers might have disappeared at different points in 1959, unable to withstand the double whammy of John's erratic behavior after his mother's death and the lack of bookings coming their way.

Slowly, things got a little better. John was comforted by the presence of Cynthia in his life. Stu helped him with his failing art school career, and Paul was finally able to get through to him as a friend who knew grief. "Now we were both in this; both losing out mothers," he recalled. "This was a bond for us, something of ours, a special thing. We'd both gone through that trauma . . . We could look at each other and know."

The truth was that while John had been the leader of his pals since he was running his Just William gang, he was dependent on his friends as well. His boyhood friend Pete Shotton observed this firsthand. "Though I have yet to encounter a personality as strong and individualistic as John's, he always had to have a partner." John took the role of ringleader as his right and reveled in being the center of attention. Yet, Pete said, "He desperately required the supportive presence of whoever he felt closest to at the time."

When John let Paul join the Quarry Men after the St. Peter's fête, there was no doubt about who had the upper hand in their relationship. Even after they became famous, the idea that John was the leader of the group persisted, and in some ways he was. But the dynamic between them was much more complicated.

On a personal level, Paul had his own insights into the relationship.

People always assume that John was the hard-edged one and I was the soft-edged one . . . John, because of his upbringing and his unstable family life, had to be hard, witty, always ready for the cover-up . . . Whereas with my rather comfortable upbringing, a lot of family . . . my surface grew to be easy-going . . . But we wouldn't have put up with each other had we each only had that surface . . . John had a lot to guard against, and it formed his personality; he was a very guarded person. I think that was the balance between us: John was caustic and witty out of necessity and, underneath, quite a warm character when you got to know him. I was the opposite, easy-going, friendly . . . but I could be tough if I needed to be.

These contradictory aspects of their personalities were also a huge part of the creative relationship. The studio engineer who recorded the Beatles' biggest albums saw all their differences behind the glass of the recording studios. The list he compiled was long. Paul was meticulous, kept a neat notebook with lyric and chord changes, and was willing to put in long hours to perfect their music. John was rude, impatient, and chaotic, always looking for scraps of paper where he'd scribbled ideas. Surprisingly, though, where Paul would take offense at criticism, John was more thick-skinned and willing to hear what others had to say.

Cynthia articulated their musical differences with sharp insight. "John needed Paul's attention to detail and persistence. Paul needed John's anarchic, lateral thinking."

It was just this creative tension, a musical yin and yang, that resulted in such a great outpouring of songs. Both Paul and John talked for years afterward about how they used their artistic differences as well as their competitive streaks to make their music better.

One example is their song "Getting Better." Paul wrote the optimistic lines, "I've got to admit it's getting better / it's getting better, all the time." When John got ahold of it, he immediately added the next harsher bit, "Can't get no worse." Paul praised this tweak as an example of something he couldn't ever have come up with by himself.

When they did write separately, hearing what the other had accomplished was a spur. After hearing John's song "Strawberry Fields Forever," his homage to the Woolton orphanage where he played as a child, Paul came back with the whimsical "Penny Lane."

As these years passed, there was less of the "nose to nose" writing that once had been the norm, but working together on a song could often turn out brilliantly. One of those songs was "Lucy in the Sky with Diamonds," written in 1966. The inspiration came from John and Cynthia's son, Julian, who was four years old at the time. He showed his father a drawing of a little girl floating through the sky, surrounded by lots of stars, and when asked what it was, Julian replied, "Lucy in the sky with diamonds." John was immediately taken with the title. Paul remembers how he showed up at John's house one day and John said, "Look at this great drawing Julian's just done." The fanciful title immediately brought them back to stories like *Through the Looking-Glass* and *The Wind in the Willows,* and they decided to use that kind of imagery in the song. "I offered cellophane flowers and newspaper taxis," Paul said, "and John replied with kaleidoscope eyes. I remember which was which because we traded words off each other as we always did."

Perhaps it's best to let Paul have the final word on their relationship. "The great thing about me and John is that it was *me and John*, end of story. Whereas everyone else can say, well, you know, he did this and so and so and so and so. The nice thing is I can actually think, 'Come on, when we got in a little room, it was *me and John* sitting down. It was me and him who wrote it, not these other people who think they know about it. I must know better than them. I was the one in the room.'"

Over the course of their songwriting life, John and Paul produced three hundred "Lennon-McCartney Originals." They made music that has been

Musical magic.

a part of people's lives for more than fifty years with no signs of winding down. Their group, the Beatles, would be named the most influential band of all time, yet would never have achieved the fame it did if it hadn't been for Lennon-McCartney's creative alchemy, which made the whole so much greater than the sum of its individual parts.

In the beginning, there were two boys growing up in war-scarred Liverpool, each pushed by family to make something respectable and proper of themselves. John Lennon and Paul McCartney came to have their own dreams, and with talent, persistence, hard work, and a little luck, those dreams came true in spectacular fashion, gracing the rest of us as well. Together, they made magic.

Not a bad legacy for two lads from Liverpool.

How the Beatles Grew Up
in Hamburg, Conquered England,
and Took the World by Storm!

JOHN, PAUL, GEORGE, Stu, and Pete Best left for Hamburg, Germany, in August of 1960 for a booking in a small nightclub, the Indra. After several more name changes, including Long John and the Silver Beetles, they had finally settled on a name: the Beatles.

There are several stories of how they finally found a name that stuck. The most common one is that John and Stu (although John sometimes said it was him alone) were looking for a name reminiscent of Buddy Holly's band, the Crickets, and came up with the name Beetles. John, with his love of language, saw that by spelling it *Beatles*, it would play off the musical term *beat*. Another version is they named themselves after a motorcycle gang, the Beetles, from the Marlon Brando movie *The Wild Ones*, which, again, John tinkered with. Either way, at long last, they had found a name for the long haul.

The Beatles had secured the Hamburg gig because of their new manager, Allan Williams, who the boys knew as the owner of the Jacaranda. Williams had gotten into the booking end of the music business, and he had a contact in Hamburg, Bruno Koschmider, who ran a string of rundown nightclubs in a sketchy part of town. The clientele at the Indra Club was a mix of locals, a few tourists, and rowdy seamen.

Williams had convinced Jim, Mimi, and the other parents involved that the boys would be well taken care of. Actually, their living conditions were awful. They were stuck rooming in a nearby movie theater's dirty storeroom, which was located next to the audience toilets. Koschmider expected the band to energetically play long shows well into the middle of the night. As the patrons drank more, fights broke out with regularity. To keep going, the Beatles started taking pills that would keep them awake. But despite all the grunge, drugs, and dangers, the five teenagers, away from England and on their own, were having the time of their lives. They expanded their skills as musicians, learned their craft as performers, and used the opportunity to play their own music, as well as American rock and blues. As George put it, "Hamburg was really like our apprenticeship, learning how to play in front of people."

In the fall of 1960, three young German people came into a large club of Bruno's, the Kaiserkeller, where the Beatles had been moved. Klaus Voorman, Jurgen Vollmer, and Astrid Kirchherr rocked the Beatles' world. The trio, like John and Stu, were art school students who were into fashion, culture, photography, and philosophy. Besides offering friendship, Klaus, Jurgen, and in particular Astrid restyled the band's image. Astrid

George, John, Paul, and Stu posing for their friend and photographer Astrid Kirchherr in a Hamburg, Germany, park.

took some of the first photographs of the Beatles, which are considered classics today. Stu was the first to "lose the Brylcreem," as Astrid put it, and she cut his hair in a short style, similar to hers, which would become the forerunner to the Beatles' signature mop-top haircuts. Soon, the other boys submitted to the scissors and began dressing in leather like their new friends. Astrid and Stu fell in love almost instantly, and by November, they were engaged.

The Beatles had several different bookings in Hamburg. After the second ended in 1961, Stu decided to stay in Hamburg with Astrid, drop music, and continue in art school there. In April 1962, the Beatles, who, by now, had a much higher musical profile in the city, were booked as the opening act in a new, large venue, the Star Club. On arrival, they learned the shocking news that Stuart Sutcliffe, after several months of headaches and blackouts, had died of a cerebral hemorrhage. Astrid was devastated, and John tried his best to help her despite his own grief.

By the end of 1961, the Beatles, thanks in part to their success in Germany, were getting better musical opportunities in England. Their most regular gig was at the Cavern Club. Having been sold and no longer a jazz bar, it was a welcoming spot for rock bands. Fans in Liverpool, especially the girls, began going wild over the Beatles. Cynthia and Dot were still John's and Paul's steadies, but that didn't mean the guys weren't getting it on with the "birds" flocking around them. Fans of both sexes were packing their shows and boosting their popularity sky-high.

One visitor to the Cavern Club was a twenty-seven-year-old named Brian Epstein. Epstein's family owned several businesses in Liverpool, and Epstein was in charge of NEMS, the North End Music Store, where, along with instruments and sheet music, records were sold—all the boys had often bought rock records there.

Part of Epstein's job was to keep up with local music. Having heard about the Beatles, he turned up for a lunchtime show at the Cavern Club on November 9, 1961. Impressed by the energy and talent he had seen onstage, he became the Beatles' manager in January of 1962. Despite no experience in this area, Epstein had many contacts in the music industry. He quickly had a huge influence on the Beatles' career. Their bookings were better, their image was enhanced, and Epstein made sure they looked and acted more professional at performances. His biggest coup, however, was securing a record contract for the Beatles with Polyphone Records in May of 1962.

The Beatles at the Cavern Club in 1963.

Perhaps the single luckiest part of this arrangement was that the contract was offered by a talented record producer, George Martin. Martin was not initially very enthusiastic about the group he had signed—and since his company wasn't paying them much, it didn't matter if they were a bust—but as he got to know the Beatles, he came to appreciate their talent and wit, and with his creative expertise as a producer and arranger, their records like *Please Please Me* and *Love Me Do* began to climb the charts. Before he signed them, however, Martin insisted the band get a new drummer. Pete Best, he felt, was not up the job. John, Paul, and

George, who had added Pete out of necessity more than affection or appreciation of his talent, insisted that Epstein step in and fire Pete. On August 16, 1962, he did, leaving Pete devastated by the decision. Ringo Starr, whom the boys knew and admired, was hired as the Beatles' drummer. They had seen him play often (and occasionally played with him), and his personality was a better fit than Pete's.

The next year was onward and upward, with the Beatles gaining fame across the UK and Europe. In November 1963, they performed in front of members of the royal family at a variety show at London's Prince of Wales Theatre. It was there John made a cheeky comment: audience members in the cheaper seats should clap while the royals could just rattle their jewelry.

On November 22, 1963, President John F. Kennedy was assassinated, shocking the United States and plunging it into gloom. Looking for something to raise the national mood, America's young people embraced the Beatles when their first album with Capitol Records, *Meet the Beatles!*, was released in the States in January 1964. John, Paul, George, and Ringo took their first trip to the United States to appear on the popular *Ed Sullivan Show* on February 9. Beatlemania, as their passionate fandom was known, moved into high gear. The Beatles quickly became a worldwide phenomenon.

Only a few years earlier, when it seemed as if their careers were going nowhere, the Beatles had a silly bit they used to do to keep their spirits up. Playing off the name of a British TV show that showcased rock, *Top of the Pops*, John would yell, "Where are we going, fellas?" And the rest of the boys would reply jokingly in fake American accents, "To the top, Johnny. To the toppermost of the poppermost."

Now they were there.

AFTERWORD

In My Life

JOHN LENNON—The years after the Beatles' international breakthrough were ones of dizzying activity both professionally and personally for John. Along with recording, touring to sold-out crowds, and songwriting, John published two books, *In His Own Write* and *A Spaniard in the Works*, full of his signature wordplay and cartooning. Along with the other Beatles, John starred in the movies *A Hard Day's Night* and *Help!* and took a solo role in *How I Won the War*. In 1962, John married a pregnant Cynthia, and their son, Julian, was born on April 8, 1963. He left his marriage in 1968 after falling in love with conceptual artist Yoko Ono. With Ono's support, John was able to explore more avant-garde artistic ventures, forming a band that was a vehicle for both their collaborative and solo efforts called the Plastic Ono Band. Together, they also became peace activists. The Beatles broke up in 1970 for professional, personal, and financial reasons. In the years after, John's musical career continued. He made a number of albums, including the critical and financial success *Imagine* in 1971. From 1975 to 1980, after the birth of his son Sean on his thirty-fifth birthday, he took on the role of primary caregiver and house husband while Yoko managed the family's extensive business holdings. His relationship with Julian was sporadic and unsatisfying for both of them. When Sean was five, John returned to the recording studio with Yoko to record an album, *Double Fantasy*, with some of the tracks chronicling his new life. On December 8, 1980, John and Yoko arrived at the Dakota, their exclusive New York City apartment building, where Mark David Chapman, a fan for whom John had earlier signed an autograph, lay in wait. As the couple walked through the building's arched driveway, Chapman pulled out a revolver and shot Lennon four times in the back. John died later that evening. He was forty years old.

PAUL McCARTNEY—After the Beatles' breakup, Paul recorded two solo albums, *McCartney* (1970) and *Ram* (1971), but realized he preferred performing in a group and didn't mind going back to square one. He formed a successful band, Wings. His wife, Linda Eastman, whom he married in 1969, joined him in the band, primarily so the family could be together. Along with Heather, Linda's daughter from a previous marriage, Paul and Linda had three other children—Mary; Stella, who became a well-known fashion designer; and James. A photographer and author of vegetarian cookbooks, Linda died in 1998 from breast cancer, the same disease that had killed Paul's mother. He then married animal rights activist Heather Mills in 2002, with whom he had one daughter, Beatrice; they divorced in 2008. Paul—now Sir Paul McCartney, having been knighted by Queen

Elizabeth II for his contribution to British culture and charity—married Nancy Shevell in 2011. Wings broke up in 1981, but Paul's musical career never stopped. He continued touring and writing songs, and he ventured into classical music. He also recorded with other musical celebrities including Michael Jackson and Elvis Costello. For years after the Beatles' acrimonious breakup, John and Paul were estranged, sometimes throwing barbs at each other through their music. In 1975, they ran into each other at a Los Angeles club and jammed a little, and the ice broke. At the time of John's death, they were friendly once again, and Paul has said he was greatly relieved that they had reconciled before John died. Paul McCartney is one of the most successful and honored musicians of all time.

GEORGE HARRISON—George's life took a decidedly more spiritual turn than his bandmates'. He became interested in Transcendental Meditation (which resulted in all four Beatles, in 1967, visiting the Maharishi Mahesh Yogi in India) and incorporated Eastern influences such as sitar music into the band's recordings. He also wrote several popular Beatles' songs, including "While My Guitar Gently Weeps" and "Something." After the breakup of the Beatles, George continued recording on his own and became a movie producer as well. In 1988, he formed the supergroup the Traveling Wilburys with Bob Dylan, Roy Orbison, Tom Petty, and Jeff Lynn. Harrison met Pattie Boyd during the filming of *A Hard Day's Night,* and they were married from 1966 to 1977. In 1978, he married Olivia Arias and had a son, Dhani, the same year. He continued his spiritual quest, and he became involved in humanitarian causes. George had started smoking when he was around age eleven and as an adult smoked two to three packs of cigarettes a day, although he quit in his later years.

After several bouts of cancer, George Harrison died of lung cancer in 2001 at age fifty-eight.

RINGO STARR—When Ringo Starr joined the Beatles in 1962, some fans resented him and picketed the Cavern Club where they often played with signs that said PETE FOREVER! RINGO NEVER! But it wasn't long before he became as popular as his bandmates. As a part of the Beatles, he sang the occasional lead on songs such as "With a Little Help from My Friends" and "Yellow Submarine" and wrote or co-wrote several songs including "Octopus's Garden." Lauded for his drumming prowess, Ringo went on to have a busy and successful musical career when the Beatles broke up, recording top-ten singles and albums, and touring with Ringo Starr & His All-Starr Band. In 2011, *Rolling Stone* magazine named Ringo Starr one of the greatest drummers of all time. He was knighted in 2018 by Queen Elizabeth II for his service to music.

MIMI SMITH—When the Beatles became famous, Mimi had to revise her opinion: John could make a living through music. However, the Beatles' success disturbed her life, as fans were continuously coming to Mendips looking for John or demanding souvenirs. In 1965, she sold Mendips, and John bought her a home by the sea in Poole, Dorset. When Mendips came on the market again, after John's death, it was purchased by Yoko Ono, who donated it to Britain's National Trust. It was made into a museum that recreates the home John lived in as boy and is visited by thousands of people from all over the world each year. Mimi outlived John by eleven years, dying in December 1991 at age eighty-five. According to the caregiver who was with her, Mimi's last words were "Hello, John."

JIM AND MICHAEL MCCARTNEY—Jim McCartney was delighted by Paul's success and in the early days would answer fan mail, pretending the letters were coming from his son. Like Mimi, however, Jim could not live a normal life with Beatles fans constantly turning up on his doorstep, so Paul bought him a Tudor-style home called the Rembrandt in a countrylike setting outside of Liverpool. In 1964, Jim married a widow, Angie Williams, and adopted her four-year-old daughter, Ruth. He died in 1976 of complications from asthma and arthritis. Michael McCartney had a successful career as a musician with several bands but eventually decided to pursue his lifelong fascination with photography. The McCartney home at 20 Forthlin Road in Liverpool was purchased by the National Trust and is labeled by the Trust as "the birthplace of the Beatles" because of the songs written there.

ALFRED LENNON—Alf stayed out of John's life until someone showed him a newspaper article about the Beatles and asked if he and John were related. In 1964, he turned up at Brian Epstein's office with a journalist. John met with him but was not interested in a relationship. Several weeks later, a down-at-the-heels Alf came to John and Cynthia's house in London. She let him in, but when John returned home, Alf was ordered out. Over the following months, John softened, and father and son forged a tentative relationship. When Alf remarried a much younger woman, Pauline, John gave her a job. Alf and Pauline had two sons, John's half brothers, who were younger than his own son, Julian. Alf wrote a manuscript about his life, explaining his side of events, which he gave to John. He died of stomach cancer in 1976. John and Alf had one last phone call in the hospital before Alf's death, ending their relationship in a place of understanding.

ENDNOTES

PROLOGUE

1. "The decision . . ." Philip Norman, *John Lennon: The Life* (New York: Ecco, 2008), 109.

CHAPTER 1: HELLO, GOODBYE

1. "such a beautiful baby . . ." Albert Goldman, *The Lives of John Lennon* (New York: William Morrow, 1988), 26.

2. "You look silly . . ." Hunter Davies, *The Beatles*, rev. ed. (New York: W. W. Norton, 2010), 5.

3. "I've done it . . ." Norman, *John Lennon*, 11.

4. The events surrounding John's decision to return home with his mother are recounted by Alfred Lennon in *Daddy, Come Home*, published in 1990, twelve years after his death, by his wife, Pauline. This is the story that is reported in almost every Lennon biography, but Mark Lewisohn, in his 2013 book, *Tune In*, includes an interview with Billy Hall, a friend of Alf's, who says he was present at the meeting between Julia and Alf and that John's fate was decided with much less drama.

CHAPTER 2: STRAWBERRY FIELDS FOREVER

1. "I remember . . ." Norman, *John Lennon*, 30.

2. "the next moment . . ." Bob Spitz, *The Beatles: The Biography* (New York: Little, Brown, 2005), 31.

3. "but she wanted John . . ." Spitz, *The Beatles*, 31.

4. The description of Mendips and John's early life there appears in *The Mendips*, a booklet published by the National Trust (UK). This information was supplemented by the author's visit to Mendips.

5. "I soon forgot my father . . ." Davies, *The Beatles*, 12.

6. "as happy as the day was long . . ." Davies, 12.

7. "Well, you couldn't have two mummies . . ." Norman, *John Lennon*, 31.

8. "You had me . . ." From the song "Mother" by John Lennon, quoted in John Lennon and Yoko Ono Lennon, *Plastic Ono Band* (Point Richmond, CA: Weldon Owen, 2020), 99.

9. "Don't 'nore me, Mimi . . ." Davies, *The Beatles*, 9.

10. "I was passionate . . ." Kevin Shortsleeve, "John Lennon: Imagining," *Recess!*, transcript of broadcast from October 9, 2002, at https://recess.ufl.edu /literature/2002/john-lennon-imagining/.

11. "'Twas brillig . . ." Lewis Carroll, "Jabberwocky," Poetry Foundation, http://www .poetryfoundation.org/poems/42916/jabberwocky.

12. "If you liked this one . . ." Davies, *The Beatles*, 10.

13. "He never had a pencil out of his hand . . ." National Trust, *The Mendips*, 13.

14. "Keep away from him . . ." Larry Kane, *When They Were Boys: The True Story of the Beatles' Rise to the Top* (Philadelphia: Running Press, 2013), 36.

15. "he'd pull me along . . ." Norman, *John Lennon*, 39.

16. "They can't hang you for it . . ." "The Playboy Interview with John Lennon and Yoko Ono," *Playboy*, January 1981.

17. "No one I think is in my tree . . ." From the song "Strawberry Fields Forever," by John Lennon, 1967.

18. "What I was trying to say . . ." "Playboy Interview."

CHAPTER 3: BAD BOYS

1. The report of John's first meeting with Pete Shotton comes in Goldman, *The Lives of John Lennon*, 48.

2. "I did not conform . . ." "Playboy Interview."

3. "Anyway . . ." "Playboy Interview."

4. "I was always so psychic . . ." "Playboy Interview."

5. "Getting the egg . . ." Pete Shotton and Nicholas Schaffner, *John Lennon: In My Life* (New York: Stein and Day, 1983), 27.

6. "I was coming down Penny Lane . . ." Davies, *The Beatles*, 11.

7. "Just like you, Mimi . . ." Davies, 11.

8. "I felt the stocking . . ." Mark Lewisohn, *Tune In*, vol. 1 of *The Beatles: All These Years* (New York: Crown Archetype, 2013), 47.

9. "He'd stay there for a week . . ." Tim Riley, *Lennon: The Man, the Myth, the Music—The Definitive Life* (New York: Hyperion, 2011), 24.

10. "John just loved the wildness . . ." Sarfraz Manzoor, "Why John Longed to Be Jock Lennon," *The Observer*, October 11, 2008, https://www.theguardian.com/music/2008/oct/12/johnlennon-scotland.

11. "He loved . . ." Manzoor, "Jock Lennon."

12. "As a kid I had a dream . . ." Lennon and Ono Lennon, *Plastic Ono Band*, 107.

13. "ivy-covered brick fortress . . ." Shotton and Schaffner, *John Lennon*, 31.

14. "What the devil is that . . ." Lennon and Ono Lennon, *Plastic Ono Band*, 33.

15. "I think the roof is leaking . . ." Lennon and Ono Lennon, 33

16. "Our sense of triumph . . ." Shotton and Schaffner, *John Lennon*, 29.

17. "It's lovely to see you . . ." Lewisohn, *Tune In*, 83.

18. "*wasted intelligence . . .*" Lewisohn, 33.

19. "I remember . . ." Davies, *The Beatles*, 15–16.

20. "the best of the five . . ." Lewisohn, *Tune In*, 77.

21. "He exasperated her . . ." Lewisohn, 44.

CHAPTER 4: MOTHER NATURE'S SON

1. "a horrible piece of red meat . . ." Davies, *The Beatles*, 23.

2. "My mother was always . . ." Barry Miles, *Paul McCartney: Many Years from Now* (New York: Henry Holt, 1997), 15.

3. "The city always ran out . . ." Miles, *Paul McCartney*, 5.

4. "If you went . . ." Paul McCartney, *The Lyrics* (New York: Liveright, 2021), 479.

5. "This is where . . ." McCartney, *Lyrics*, 10.

6. "So when I got into the woods . . ." McCartney, 11.

7. "virtually a door-to-door salesman . . ." McCartney, 8.

8. "I was not shy . . ." McCartney, 8.

9. "There was quite a musical atmosphere . . ." Paul Du Noyer, *Conversations with McCartney* (New York: Overlook Press, 2016), 15.

10. "you'll always be invited . . ." Du Noyer, *Conversations*, 15.

CHAPTER 5: PENNY LANE

1. "I have a crystal-clear memory . . ." Miles, *Paul McCartney*, 6.

2. "It was out of gratitude . . ." Davies, *The Beatles*, 24.

3. "'That was nice of you . . .'" Du Noyer, *Conversations*, 9.

4. "There's one moment . . ." Miles, *Paul McCartney*, 15.

5. "I was pretty sneaky . . ." Davies, *The Beatles*, 24.

6. "He was very into crosswords . . ." Spitz, *The Beatles*, 82.

7. "Put it there . . ." Du Noyer, *Conversations*, 20.

8. "a very intelligent boy . . ." Philip Norman, *Paul McCartney: The Life* (New York: Little, Brown, 2016), 25.

9. "my knees went rubbery . . ." Miles, *Paul McCartney*, 7.

10. "I was shaking . . ." Lewisohn, *Tune In*, 63.

11. "You were born not for yourself . . ." Spitz, *The Beatles*, 83.

12. "Then, we got interested in the other bits . . ." Howard Sounes, *Fab: An Intimate*

Life of Paul McCartney (New York: Da Capo, 2010), 14.

13. "He had this angelic-type face . . ." Norman, *Paul McCartney*, 33–34.

14. "We used to sit . . ." Miles, *Paul McCartney*, 15.

15. "There was a barber shop called Bioletti's . . ." Miles, 307.

16. "[I] couldn't figure out at all how to play it . . ." Miles, 21.

17. "Now everything's ready . . ." Spitz, *The Beatles*, 89.

18. "My mother's death . . ." "Paul McCartney's Mother Mary Dies," The Beatles Bible, https://www.beatlesbible.com/1956/10/31/paul-mccartneys-mother-mary-dies/.

CHAPTER 6: GOTTA BE ROCK-AND-ROLL MUSIC

1. "I remember . . ." David Pritchard and Alan Lysaght, *The Beatles: An Oral History* (New York: Hyperion, 1998), 13.

2. "first hit me . . . their humor . . . Hipper than . . ." John Lennon, review of "The Goon Show Scripts," *The New York Times*, 1972, transcribed in *The Goon Show* Site, http://www.thegoonshow.net/tributes/john_lennon.asp.

3. "I had no idea . . ." "Playboy Interview."

4. "There wasn't nobody playing . . ." Philip Lewis, "Who Invented Rock 'n' Roll? These Are the Black Pioneers Who Laid the Genre's Foundations," *Mic*, March 7, 2016, https://www.mic.com/articles/136969/who-invented-rock-n-roll -these-are-the-black-pioneers-who-laid-the-genre-s-foundations.

5. "To us it just sounded like . . ." Lewisohn, *Tune In*, 89.

6. "The Messiah had arrived . . ." Spitz, *The Beatles*, 41.

7. "stopped in his tracks . . ." Lewisohn, *Tune In*, 89.

8. "His reaction that day . . ." Lewisohn, 89.

9. "How could this be happening . . ." Lewisohn, 90.

10. "Little Richard was this voice . . ." Lewisohn, 103.

11. "They're the same pair . . ." Norman, *Paul McCartney*, 43.

12. "A fashion leader . . ." Shotton and Schaffner, *John Lennon*, 50.

13. "I was never really a street kid . . ." Shotton and Schaffner, 50.

14. "Our fifteenth birthdays . . ." Spitz, *The Beatles*, 36.

15. "I think I had one lesson . . ." The Beatles, *The Beatles Anthology* (San Francisco: Chronicle Books, 2000), 11.

16. "Why don't we . . ." Shotton and Schaffner, *John Lennon*, 51.

17. "Since our native Woolton . . ." Shotton and Schaffner, 53.

18. "minding their manners . . ." Spitz, *The Beatles*, 54.

19. "We discovered Gene Vincent there . . ." Spitz, 55.

20. "Julia was unlike anyone . . ." Spitz, 55.

21. "So it was off to his mum's . . ." Spitz, 55.

22. "It was right there at his fingertips . . ." Spitz, 51.

CHAPTER 7: COME TOGETHER

1. "The guitar's all very well . . ." Shotton and Schaffner, *John Lennon*, 51.

2. "I was always thinking . . ." The Beatles, *The Beatles Anthology*, 12.

3. "I learned to cook . . ." The Beatles, 20.

4. "The minute he got the guitar . . ." Davies, *The Beatles*, 31.

5. "We used to go around . . ." Davies, 31.

6. "John reacted . . ." Spitz, *The Beatles*, 60.

7. "John was very witty that night . . ." Spitz, 61.

8. "Come Go with Me." Song recorded by the Del-Vikings, 1956, written by C. E. Quick.

9. "John and Paul circled . . ." Spitz, *The Beatles*, 97.

10. "I saw him a few times . . ." Lewisohn, *Tune In*, 130.

11. "I was just on the wrong side . . ." Lewisohn, 130.

12. "He gave a great performance . . ." Norman, *Paul McCartney*, 50.

13. "also the Quarry Men . . ." From the St. Peter's fête program, obtained by the author in Liverpool.

14. "Well, Pete . . ." Shotton and Schaffner, *John Lennon*, 55.

15. "I've been talking . . ." Shotton and Schaffner, 55.

16. "He wrote pages . . ." "Barbara Baker," The Beatle Girls Site, http://sentstarr
    .tripod.com/beatgirls/baker.html.

17. "Kids of John's and my generation . . ." Shotton and Schaffner, *John Lennon*, 9.

18. The story of Pete and the tin washboard is told in Shotton and Schaffner, 7–8.

CHAPTER 8: YOU REALLY GOT A HOLD ON ME

1. "cabbage and boiled grasshoppers," The Beatles, *The Beatles Anthology*, 30.

2. "I should have been an illustrator . . ." The Beatles, 13.

3. "John Lennon striding around . . ." Lewisohn, *Tune In*, 143.

4. "For you to be a teenage boy . . ." Miles, *Paul McCartney*, 48.

5. "John, your little friend . . ." Sounes, *Fab*, 24.

6. "He'll get you into trouble, son . . ." Lewisohn, *Tune In*, 148.

7. "By a million-to-one chance . . ." Lewisohn, 148.

8. "For my first gig . . ." The Beatles, *The Beatles Anthology*, 21.

9. "At first, we were embarrassed . . ." Spitz, *The Beatles*, 109.

10. "I could only play . . ." The Beatles, *The Beatles Anthology*, 12.

11. "I was riding along . . ." Lewisohn, *Tune In*, 89.

12. "I would sit around for hours . . ." The Beatles, *The Beatles Anthology*, 28.

13. "I didn't dig him . . ." Spitz, *The Beatles*, 27, and Lewisohn, *Tune In*, 158, both
    quote John on his reaction to meeting George.

14. "You always seem to like the lower-class types . . ." Spitz, 48.

15. "All I ever wanted to do . . ." Lewisohn, *Tune In*, 158.

16. "He had a great sense of himself . . ." Lewisohn, 158.

17. "I was asked by John to join . . ." Lewisohn, 158.

18. "He was very sarcastic . . ." Lewisohn, 159.

19. "I remember we all went down on the bus . . ." "Recording: In Spite of All the

Danger, That'll Be the Day," The Beatles Bible, https://www.beatlesbible
.com/1958/07/12/recording-in-spite-of-all-the-danger-thatll-be-the-day/,
quoting Mark Lewisohn, *The Beatles Recording Sessions: The Official Abbey
Road Studio Session Notes, 1962–1970* (New York: Harmony Books, 1989).

CHAPTER 9: LET IT BE

1. "I was staying . . ." Davies, *The Beatles*, 48.

2. "We got a taxi . . ." Davies, 48.

3. "Mimi said John was out . . ." Lewisohn, *Tune In*, 181.

4. According to Mark Lewisohn, this account of Julia's last visit with Mimi was
discovered in Mimi's personal papers after her death, which occurred eleven
years after John's murder. It is assumed John never knew about it since he
never mentioned it.

5. "There was Julia . . ." Lewisohn, 181.

6. "John and I . . ." Lewisohn, 182.

7. "If anything like that happened to me . . ." Lewisohn, 172.

8. "Sorry about your mum . . ." Shotton and Schaffner, *John Lennon*, 61.

9. "Don't blame me . . ." Lewisohn, *Tune In*, 208.

10. "I was absolutely amazed . . ." Spitz, *The Beatles*, 139.

11. "This lineup may at first . . ." Norman, *Paul McCartney*, 72.

CHAPTER 10: I'M DOWN

1. "Julia was the light of John's life . . ." Miles, *Paul McCartney*, 48.

2. "I was quite a lone wolf . . ." Miles, 42.

3. "I was in a sort of blind rage . . ." Davies, *The Beatles*, 53.

4. "He was full of contradictions and confusion . . ." Cynthia Lennon, *John* (London:
Hodder and Stoughton, 2005), 34.

5. "about three hundred people . . ." Cynthia Lennon, *John*, 84.

CHAPTER 11: THE LONG AND WINDING ROAD

1. "One day . . ." McCartney, *Lyrics*, 570.

2. "Physically, it was always a bad idea . . ." Miles, *Paul McCartney*, 46.

3. "sagging off . . ." Miles, 34.

4. "We had to waft . . ." The Beatles, *The Beatles Anthology*, 23.

5. "nose to nose . . ." Spitz, *The Beatles*, 133.

6. "Because I was left-handed . . ." Miles, *Paul McCartney*, 36.

7. "We'd sit down . . ." Lewisohn, *Tune In*, 11.

8. "It was great . . ." The Beatles, *The Beatles Anthology*, 23.

9. "And Paul hits this chord . . ." "Yeah! Yeah! Yeah!" *The Observer*, February 1, 2004,
   https://www.theguardian.com/music/2004/feb/01/thebeatles.popandrock.

10. "We couldn't quite figure out . . ." Norman, *John Lennon*, 121.

11. "Jumble Jim . . ." Lewisohn, *Tune In*, 194.

12. "Now we were both in this . . ." Spitz, *The Beatles*, 147.

13. "Though I have yet to encounter . . ." Shotton and Schaffner, *John Lennon*, 21.

14. "He desperately required . . ." Shotton and Schaffner, 52.

15. "People always assume . . ." Miles, *Paul McCartney*, 31–32.

16. Thoughts on the Beatles' working relationship. Joshua Wolf Shenk, "The Power
   of Two," *The Atlantic*, July/August 2014.

17. "John needed . . ." Cynthia Lennon, *John*, 45.

18. "Look at this great drawing . . ." The Beatles, *The Beatles Anthology*, 242.

19. "The great thing about me and John . . ." Du Noyer, *Conversations with
   McCartney*, 160.

CHAPTER 12: HOW THE BEATLES GREW UP IN HAMBURG, CONQUERED ENGLAND, AND TOOK THE WORLD BY STORM!

1. "Hamburg was really . . ." The Beatles, *The Beatles Anthology*, 48.

2. "Where are we going . . ." Lewisohn, *Tune In*, 157.

BIBLIOGRAPHY

BOOKS

The Beatles. *The Beatles Anthology*. San Francisco: Chronicle Books, 2000.

Blaney, John. *John Lennon: In His Life*. New York: WhiteStar, 2009.

Carlin, Peter Ames. *Paul McCartney: A Life*. New York: Simon & Schuster/Touchstone, 2009.

Davies, Hunter. *The Beatles*. Rev. ed. New York: W. W. Norton, 2010.

Davies, Hunter, editor. *The John Lennon Letters*. New York: Little, Brown, 2012.

Du Noyer, Paul. *Conversations with McCartney*. New York: Overlook Press, 2016.

Giuliano, Geoffrey. *Two of Us: John Lennon & Paul McCartney, Behind the Myth*. New York: Penguin, 1999.

Goldman, Albert. *The Lives of John Lennon*. New York: William Morrow, 1988.

Hajeski, Nancy J. *The Beatles: Here, There, and Everywhere*. San Diego: Thunder Bay Press, 2014.

Jones, Ron. *The Beatles' Liverpool: The Complete Guide*. Liverpool: Liverpool History Press, 2014.

Kane, Larry. *When They Were Boys: The True Story of the Beatles' Rise to the Top*. Philadelphia: Running Press, 2013.

Leigh, Spencer. *The Beatles in Liverpool: The Stories, the Scene, and the Path to Stardom*. Chicago: Chicago Review Press, 2012.

Lennon, Cynthia. *John*. London: Hodder and Stoughton, 2005.

Lennon, John, and Yoko Ono. *Plastic Ono Band*. Richmond Point, CA: Weldon Owen, 2020.

Lewisohn, Mark. *The Beatles Recording Sessions: The Official Abbey Road Studio Session Notes, 1962–1970*. New York: Harmony Books, 1989.

Lewisohn, Mark. *The Complete Beatles Chronicles*. New York: Harmony Books, 1982.

Lewisohn, Mark. *Tune In*, volume 1 of *The Beatles: All These Years*. New York: Crown Archetype, 2013.

McCartney, Michael. *Remember: The Recollections and Photographs of the Beatles*. New York: Henry Holt, 1992.

McCartney, Paul. *The Lyrics*. New York: Liveright, 2021.

Miles, Barry. *Paul McCartney: Many Years from Now*. New York: Henry Holt, 1997.

National Trust. *20 Forthlin Road, Allerton, Liverpool*. London: National Trust Enterprises, 1998; rev. ed, 2009.

National Trust. *Mendips*. London: National Trust Enterprises, 2003.

Norman, Philip. *John Lennon: The Life*. New York: Ecco, 2008.

Norman, Philip. *Paul McCartney: The Life*. New York: Little, Brown, 2016.

Partridge, Elizabeth. *John Lennon: All I Want Is the Truth*. New York: Viking, 2005.

Pritchard, David, and Alan Lysaght. *The Beatles: An Oral History*. New York: Hyperion, 1998.

Riley, Tim. *Lennon: The Man, the Myth, the Music—The Definitive Life*. New York: Hyperion, 2011.

Roach, Kevin. *Julia*. Liverpool: Beatles Liverpool and More Publishing, 2014.

Shea, Stuart, and Robert Rodriguez. *Fab Four FAQ*. New York: Hal Leonard Books, 2007.

Sheff, David. *All We Are Saying: The Last Major Interview with John Lennon and Yoko Ono*. New York: St. Martin's/Griffin, 2000.

Shotton, Pete, and Nicholas Shaffner. *John Lennon: In My Life*. New York: Stein and Day, 1983.

Solt, Andrew, and Sam Egan. *Imagine: John Lennon*. New York: Macmillan, 1988.

Sounes, Howard. *Fab: An Intimate Life of Paul McCartney*. New York: Da Capo, 2010.

Spitz, Bob. *The Beatles: The Biography*. New York: Little, Brown, 2005.

MAGAZINES

The Beatles Are Back. Macfadden-Bartell Corporation, 1964.

"The Beginnings of the Beatles." Edited by Bill Harry. *Mersey Beat* 1, no. 13, 1962.

Paul. Special issue of *Life Magazine*, 2014.

"The Playboy Interview with John Lennon and Yoko Ono." Interview by David Sheff. *Playboy*, January 1981.

Remembering John Lennon. Special issue of *Life Magazine*, 2016.

Shenk, Joshua Wolf. "The Power of Two." *The Atlantic*, July/August 2014.

WEBSITES

The Beatles Bible. beatlesbible.com

Beatles Liverpool and More. beatlesliverpoolandmore.com

CultureSonar. culturesonar.com

The Goon Show Site. thegoonshow.net

The Guardian. theguardian.com

Mic. mic.com

The Poetry Foundation. poetryfoundation.org

Recess! recess.ufl.edu

TELEVISION SHOWS

The Late Late Show with James Corden. "Eight Days a Week," segment with Paul
   McCartney in the feature "Carpool Karaoke," June 21, 2018.

The author (center) and Ginny Venson Grenier (left) at the 1964 Beatles
concert in Chicago, Illinois.

AUTHOR'S NOTE

I WAS IN high school when the Beatles' first album with Capitol Records, *Meet the Beatles!*, was released in the United States in January 1964. I gave a friend the album that month as a birthday present, and she returned it because she didn't know who the Beatles were. After the Beatles appeared on *The Ed Sullivan Show* a few weeks later, everyone knew who they were (and my friend rushed out to buy the record).

That there would still be interest in the lives and music of John Lennon and Paul McCartney sixty years after their appearance on *The Ed Sullivan Show* was certainly not a given. Yet new books about Lennon and McCartney in particular and the Beatles in general come out almost every publishing season. If you are lucky enough, as I was, to visit Liverpool and see the places that formed them, you will find yourself surrounded by fellow fans of all ages from all over the world.

When I write a biography, I try to understand what mix of personality, upbringing, ambition, talent, and serendipity brings someone to the forefront. Every person of achievement was once a young person with hopes and dreams, fears and problems, just like the readers of my books. I like to think they see themselves in the familiar faces I write about—and begin wondering about what their own stories may hold.

ACKNOWLEDGMENTS

THREE PEOPLE DESERVE my special thanks for helping make this book a reality: Ken Wright, former president and publisher of Viking and Philomel Books, for his guidance, patience, and always his friendship. Howard Reeves, an extraordinary editor with a keen eye and the ability to move along my writing with just the right amounts of push and pull. Last, but hardly least, my husband, Bill Ott, who is always asking, "How can I help you?" He does, every day, in every way—but special thanks, Bill, for organizing the always-tricky notes!

At Viking, I owe huge thanks to Claire Tattersfield, who was helpful, patient, and supportive in equal measure. And thank you to Jim Hoover for his creative design. Viking has amazing copyeditors: Bethany Bryan, Marinda Valenti, Megan Zid, Krista Ahlberg, and Sola Akinlana.

Photo researcher Clare Maxwell's resourceful diligence hunting down photographs is much appreciated.

I'd also like to thank the people of Liverpool, who shared stories and took me to out-of-the-way places, and the fans who host Beatles websites, especially Kevin Roach of Beatles Liverpool and More.

Index

Note: Italicized page numbers indicate material in tables or illustrations.

PHOTOGRAPHY CREDITS

Ilene Cooper is the author of more than thirty books for young people, including *The Golden Rule, Jack: The Early Years of John F. Kennedy,* and the Absolutely Lucy series. The Illinois Reading Council named Cooper the Prairie State Award winner for Excellence in Writing for Children. She is the winner of the Jewish Book Council Award for *Jewish Holidays All Year Round,* and has received numerous accolades from review journals and social studies organizations. You can visit her online at IleneCooper.com.